⟨ **W9-CGT-908**

Living with a
Cockatiel

Edited by Neil A. Forbes

BARRON'S

ACKNOWLEDGMENTS

The publisher would like to thank the following for help with photography: Simon Goodman, Aber Birds (http://www.aberbirds.co.uk/index.html); Craig Harris, UK Parrot Cages; and Dottie Kennedy. Page 2 © istockphoto.com/Tomislav Stajduhar; Page 10 © istockphoto.com/Peter Hibberd; Page 14 © istockphoto.com/Scott Winegarden; Page 16 © istockphoto.com/David Morch; Page 42 © istockphoto.com/Lee Feldstein; Page 58 © istockphoto.com/P. J. Jones; Page 70 © istockphoto.com/David Morch; Page 73 © istockphoto.com/Eu Toch; Page 77 © istockphoto.com/David Morch; Page 82 © istockphoto.com/David Morch; Page 83 © istockphoto.com/EuToch; Page 88 © istockphoto.com/David Morch; Page 96 © istockphoto.com/Christoph Riddle; Page 100 © istockphoto.com/Johanna Goodyear; Page 101 © istockphoto.com/David Morch. Back cover photograph © istockphoto.com/Peter Hibberd. Thanks are also due to: Chris Hardwick; Maureen Cranston; Athena Jeske, Cedric B and family; Carol Erkins; Nicole Johnson; Shobana Appavu; and Linda Greeson.

First edition for the United States and Canada published in 2007 by Barron's Educational Series, Inc.

First published in Great Britain in 2007 by Ringpress Books

All inquiries should be addressed to:
Barron's Educational Series, Inc.
250 Wireless Boulevard
Hauppauge, NY 11788
www.barronseduc.com

Library of Congress Control Number: 2005934492
ISBN-13: 978-0-7641-5956-5
ISBN-10: 0-7641-5956-9

Printed in Singapore
9 8 7 6 5 4 3 2 1

CONTENTS

CHAPTER ONE

INTRODUCING THE COCKATIEL

Gentle, companionable, cheeky, and beautiful to look at, the cockatiel is the second most popular pet bird in the world, with only the ubiquitous parakeet (known in the U.K. as the budgerigar) beating it to first place. The cockatiel certainly has plenty to recommend it:

- *It is a hardy bird and suffers from few health problems.*
  The cockatiel is one of the easiest birds to keep as a pet, and will thrive as long as you provide suitable housing and the correct diet.
- *Cockatiels come in a variety of different colors.*
  The cockatiel is an attractive bird, and although it does not have as many color varieties as the parakeet, there are still plenty to choose from.
- *Cockatiels like to chatter, but they do not make as much noise some of the other species of parrot.*
  Some pet birds, particularly larger parrots, can be very noisy and piercing on occasion.

- *A cockatiel that is well looked after will live for 20 years or more.*
  This is the average life expectancy, but there are records of some cockatiels living to their late twenties.
- *Cockatiels are a handy size for pet birds.*
  A cockatiel is larger than a parakeet, reaching an adult size of around 12 inches (30 cm), which makes it easy to handle, but it does not need as much living space as some of the larger members of the parrot family.
- *Cockatiels are sociable birds.*
  They live peacefully with their own kind, and they also mix well with other birds.
- *Cockatiels are intelligent and enjoy being trained.*
  A cockatiel can be taught to perform tricks. It also has a talent for mimicry and can learn to talk and to whistle tunes.
- *Most cockatiels form a close bond with their owners.*
  The more time you spend with your cockatiel, the more it will relate to you.

Cockatiels are among the most popular of all pet birds.

ANCESTORS OF BIRDS

Birds are among the most successful creatures that inhabit the earth. There are more than 9,000 different species of birds that live all over the world, adapting to different climatic and environmental conditions. They are all descended from a crow-sized creature called Archaeopteryx. Its fossil remains, which date back 150 million years, show that Archaeopteryx was covered in feathers and would have been able to fly.

IN THE WILD

Wild cockatiels are mostly gray birds and are generally smaller than the domestic cockatiels we keep as pets. They live alongside creeks in areas of grass and scrub growth, and can survive in semi-desert conditions. When food and water are scarce, they take to the wing and live a nomadic existence, moving from place to place in search of food and water.

The color of their plumage, which varies between light and dark gray, with a white band

THE BIRD MAN

The cockatiel originally comes from Australia. Little was known about this bird until British naturalist John Gould went to Australia with the specific intention of identifying the fauna of this distant land.

Born in 1804, John received no formal education but was always keenly interested in wildlife. It seemed that he would follow in his father's footsteps and become a gardener, and, at the age of 14, he was apprenticed at Kew Gardens. But after a short spell working at Ripley Castle in Yorkshire, John moved to London in 1822 where he gave up gardening and took up taxidermy, which is the art of on the wings, blends in with the Australian grassland. Head markings include a yellow mask, red cheek patches, and a small crest. Cockatiels are dimorphic: the male "cock" has more vivid coloring than the female "hen."

Cockatiels generally fly in flocks, numbering around 50 birds. However, flocks of thousands of cockatiels may congregate at a watering place. Cockatiels have the distinction of being Australia's fastest-flying birds. Unlike other small parrots that have an undulating flight, the cockatiel's flight is even, fast, and straight. They

preparing the skins of dead animals so they appear lifelike. In 1827 he became the curator of the newly formed Zoological Society, and here he dealt with many of the newly discovered specimens that were sent in from collectors around the world.

During this period John met his future wife, Elizabeth, who was a talented artist. Together they learned the art of lithography. This is a special printing process using a plate on which only the image to be printed takes up the ink. Their published work, *A Century of Birds From the Himalayan Mountains*, has illustrations and accurate scientific descriptions of hundreds of birds. *Birds of Europe* followed, and John became famous, known everywhere as "the birdman."

Next he turned his attention to Australia. John's brothers-in-law had emigrated to Australia in the early 1830s, and they had sent back "strange and unusual specimens." John decided to attempt a classification of the animals found in this faraway land. He made a start on a book, *The Birds of Australia*, but it soon became clear that he did not have sufficient specimens to create a comprehensive reference. He

decided there was no option but to go on an expedition to Australia so he could record the wildlife for himself.

John set sail for Australia in 1938 with his wife, his eldest son, and his collector, John Gilbert. For the next 19 months he dedicated himself to collecting as much information as he could about the fauna of Australia. Enduring terrible conditions, including one of Australia's worst droughts, John Gould worked tirelessly, observing bird and mammal life and collecting specimens.

Of the estimated 745 species of birds that live in Australia, John Gould is credited with describing almost half—many of them species that had never been heard of previously. From sketches in the field, color lithographs were prepared—many produced by Elizabeth—and the end result, *Birds of Australia*, remains a landmark in ornithology.

John Gould was the first to give an accurate scientific description of the cockatiel, which was then known as the corella. There is a lithograph of a cockatiel, made by the Goulds in 1840, which appeared in Volume X of *The Naturalist Library*.

In the wild, the cockatiel flies at great speed so that it can escape from birds of prey.

use their speed to escape from birds of prey, which are their greatest enemy in the wild. For this reason, they prefer to perch in high places so they can get a good view and spot potential predators.

Wild cockatiels come down to the ground to feed. They live on grasses and plants, grain, fruits, and berries. But these little birds are very vulnerable when they are on the ground, as their vision is obscured by scrub and grasses. House cats that have become feral see cockatiels as easy pickings, and they have become a major threat to the cockatiel population.

For seed-loving cockatiels, crops are an irresistible source of food. One small cockatiel will not do much damage, but a large flock can wreak havoc. As a result, farmers view wild cockatiels as a major menace, and many wild birds are destroyed because of the damage they cause to farm crops.

The breeding season depends on the rainfall—there must be a plentiful supply of food and water when the chicks are hatched. Cockatiels in the wild generally nest between August and December, using the hollows in trees as ready-made nests. They lay four to seven eggs on a bed of decayed wood dust in the bottom of the hollow. It takes 21 to 23 days to incubate the eggs. Young birds leave the nest and become independent when they are four to five weeks of age.

Parakeets also come from Australia, and they share a similar lifestyle to cockatiels. For this reason, cockatiels will live very happily alongside parakeets if they are kept in an aviary. In fact, many bird keepers have reported close friendships between parakeets and cockatiels.

WHAT'S IN A NAME?

The name "cockatiel" comes from the Dutch word "kakatielje," which means "little cockatoo."

Its scientific name is *Nymphicus hollandicus*. "Nymphicus" means "like a nymph." "Hollandicus" refers to the country of origin: Australia was known as New Holland at the time the cockatiel was named.

Throughout its history, the cockatiel has been known by different common and scientific names. Here are some of them:

- Corella
- Crested Ground Parakeet
- Gray Parrot
- Yellow Top-knotted Parrot
- Cockatoo Parrot
- Cockateel

In Australia today, the cockatiel might be called a Quarrion or a Top-knot Parakeet. Aborigines know it as Weero. In the United States, the shorthand form of Tiel is often used.

IN CAPTIVITY

Raising cockatiels is a pleasurable and relaxing hobby. They are an attractive species, with a friendly and adaptable personality. If you have a love of birds and cockatiels in particular, then you have the essentials to be a true cockatiel fancier.

It is not known exactly how the cockatiel found its way to Europe, but there is a record that cockatiels were on display in the famous Jardin des Plantes in Paris in 1846. They were bred in captivity in Germany in 1850, and in 1863 London Zoo bred its first family of cockatiels.

To begin with, keeping pet birds was a hobby for the wealthy. By the late 1800s, it was fashionable for a large house to have an aviary, and cockatiels, which were easy to keep, were a popular choice.

Bird keepers found that cockatiels bred readily in captivity, and so it was relatively easy to establish a breeding colony. Interest in the species became widespread; in 1910 the United States reported its first breeding pair of cockatiels, and a decade later, cockatiels were reported to be breeding as far afield as India and Japan.

WHAT MAKES A PARROT A PARROT?

The cockatiel is a member of the parrot family, a rich and diverse group with approximately 358 different species. All species with parrotlike features come under the order of Psittaciformes. Shared features among parrots include

- A curved, rounded upper beak, which covers a smaller, cup-shaped lower beak. This varies in size from species to species, depending on

Features shared by all members of the parrot family.

Craniofacial hinge

Curved upper beak covering a cup-shaped lower beak

Fleshy tongue

Zygodactyl feet

• Intelligence. Parrots can be taught to perform tricks, and they are also problem-solvers.
• Mimicry. Parrots have the ability to copy all types of sounds from engines to human speech. This ability is more evident in males.
• Zygodactyl feet. Parrots have two toes pointing forward and two toes pointing back. Most species of bird have three toes forward and one back. This allows parrots to be far more dextrous; they can pick up objects and manipulate them, as well as being good climbers.

IDENTITY CRISIS

The parrot family is subdivided into three smaller groups:

Psittacidae: The true parrots, including Parrots, Parakeets, and Macaws. There are 259 species in this group.
Loriidae: This includes the Lories and Lorikeets, and numbers 55 species.
Cacatuidae: The 18 species of Cockatoo, including the cockatiel.

diet, but the basic shape is shared by all members of the parrot family.
• A craniofacial hinge. In most birds, the beak is attached directly to the head. But parrots have an extra joint between the upper beak and the skull, known as the craniofacial hinge, which allows for a far greater degree of movement.
• A thick, fleshy tongue that is highly mobile. Parrots use their tongues far more than other birds when they are ingesting food.
• A large, broad head and a short neck.

There has been some debate as to whether the cockatiel belongs with the Parrot group, related to Parakeets, or with the Cockatoo group.

Cockatoos are larger, more flamboyant birds, but the cockatiel has a crest of feathers on the top of its head, which is a feature of all Cockatoos. Cockatiels also share many of the same behavioral traits with Cockatoos, such as both parents being involved in incubation and parenting duties. In terms of appearance, the cockatiel bears a strong resemblance to Parakeets, with a similar body structure and tail feather length, and it is also a powerful flyer. However, recent research, including DNA testing, shows that the cockatiel has its strongest links with Cockatoos.

CHANGING TIMES

By the early 1900s cockatiels were being kept and bred by an increasing number of people, although they were still quite expensive. A good pair of cockatiels cost around $5.50 to $7.50, which was a lot of money at the time. Poor-quality birds could be imported at a lower price, but, generally, it was only dedicated bird fanciers who could afford to keep cockatiels. Interestingly, the larger and more exotic species of parrot, such as Amazon Grays and Amazons, could be bought far more cheaply, and these species flooded the market in the 1950s.

However, the situation was to change dramatically in 1959 when the Australian government imposed a ban on exporting its fauna to the rest of the world. Within a few years, other countries followed the Australian

FAMILY LINKS

It is now thought that cockatiels have the closest links with Cockatoos, and therefore belong in the Cacatuidae group.

Greater Sulphur-Crested Cockatoo: All Cockatoos have a crest of feathers on their heads, which is a feature shared by cockatiels.

The cockatiel shares many behavioral traits with Cockatoos.

- In the classification of animals, birds are classed as **aves**.
- Matters relating to birds, or the characteristics of birds, are referred to as **avian**.
- The practice of bird keeping is known as **aviculture**.
- A bird keeper is known as an **aviculturist**.

example, and the price of parrots soared. People who wanted pet birds turned their attention to the smaller parrots that would breed in captivity. By the late 1960s, the small parakeets of South America, the lovebirds of Africa, and the cockatiel were the most popular pets.

Since that time, the cockatiel has gained ground on the other species, and it is only the parakeet that can rival its immense popularity.

THE RIGHT CHOICE

It is tempting to rush into pet ownership, but the cockatiel, like all birds, has its special needs, and it is important that you weigh the pros and cons before making your first purchase.

The first consideration is housing. Do you intend to keep your birds in an outside aviary, or do you want pet birds living in the house? Obviously, this has implications in terms of space and cost (see Chapter 3). Generally, pet owners prefer to keep their cockatiels in the home, and those who breed and exhibit cockatiels, and have larger numbers, will choose an aviary. If you are planning to establish an aviary, your birds will have other birds for company. Cockatiels are sociable creatures, and if you are keeping a single pet bird in the house, you will need to provide companionship and mental stimulation so that your tiel is happily occupied.

Once you have made up your mind that bird keeping is for you—and the cockatiel is your preferred choice—you can make your home ready, and then go out and choose your cockatiels. If you have made all the right preparations, it is a decision you will never regret, as the cockatiel is, without a doubt, one of the most rewarding of all birds to keep in your home.

A tame cockatiel will form a close bond with its owner.

CHAPTER TWO

CHOOSING A COCKATIEL

Before you buy a cockatiel, you will need to decide on the color and sex of the bird. You will then need to find a cockatiel breeder or a pet store that has a reputation for selling sound, healthy birds. Cockatiels are relatively inexpensive to buy and you should have no problem locating pet stores or breeders in your area.

If you will be using a pet store, it is worth taking a visit before you buy your birds so you can check it out. There are many places that specialize in birds rather then being a general pet store, and you may well find that this type of store is more suitable for your needs, even if you have to travel further. A specialist avian store will generally have knowledgeable staff who will be able to give you good advice. The birds will be obtained from reputable sources, and they will be looked after properly while in the store. Have a look around the premises and check that the birds are kept in clean, hygienic conditions. Talk to the staff, and see if they are

knowledgeable about bird keeping. If you are not happy with what you find, do not go ahead with your purchase. It is vitally important that you get a good start in your bird-keeping career; taking on a bird that may be in poor condition could be disastrous.

If you are interested in a particular color, or you are looking for a bird of show quality, you will need to go to a special breeder and you should expect to pay more. The Internet has details of local and national breeders, or you can buy an avian magazine with advertisements of birds for sale.

WHAT TO LOOK FOR

How can you tell if a cockatiel is fit and healthy? If possible, seek the assistance of an experienced bird keeper who can help you make your choice. Here are some guidelines to follow:

- Ideally, you want a cockatiel aged seven to eight weeks that is fully weaned. You also need

to find out how the birds have been reared, as you want a cockatiel that has been hand-fed and is used to being handled.

- A healthy bird should be active, alert, and interested in everything that is going on.
- The body should be well-covered; it should not appear bloated or bony.
- The feathers should be clean and smooth and lie flat to the body. Puffed-out feathers and a drooping tail indicate poor health. Baby birds can sometimes look a little shabby as a result of playing, but this is nothing to worry about as long as other indicators of good health are apparent.
- There should be no bald patches or signs of parasites. To inspect the skin, blow lightly to part the feathers. The skin should look healthy. Beware of red skin, or skin that is dry or flaky.

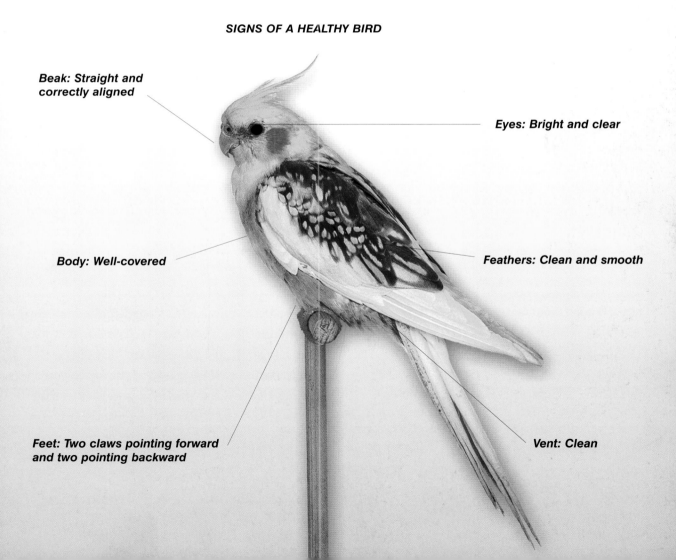

SIGNS OF A HEALTHY BIRD

Beak: Straight and correctly aligned

Eyes: Bright and clear

Body: Well-covered

Feathers: Clean and smooth

Feet: Two claws pointing forward and two pointing backward

Vent: Clean

- Cockatiels generally rest on one foot, so you should take this as a good sign.
- The cockatiel should be able to grip the perch with ease; it will find this difficult if its claws are overgrown or if it has missing claws. Check that all claws (two pointing forward and two pointing backward on each foot) are present.
- The beak should be straight and correctly aligned so the upper and lower portions meet. If the beak is misaligned, the beak will not wear down and will become misshapen or grow too long.
- The eyes should be bright and clear. Dull, vacant eyes often indicate poor health.
- The vent (under the tail) should be clean.
- Breathing should be quiet with no wheezing.

AGE TEST

How can you be sure that you are buying a young cockatiel? Hopefully the breeder or pet storekeeper will be able to give you accurate information, but look out for the following signs that are characteristic of a young bird:

Cockatiels enjoy each other's company, but a single bird will bond more closely with its owner.

- The cere (the flesh above the beak) is still pink.
- The cheek spots are apparent, but not brightly colored.
- The tail may be slightly shorter than in a full-grown cockatiel.
- Tail feathers have thin white/yellow edges.

WING CLIPPING

This procedure, carried out by many aviculturists, inhibits a cockatiel's ability to fly. The pros and cons of wing clipping are discussed in Chapter 6, but at this stage you should find out if the cockatiel you intend to buy has had its wings clipped. Ideally, a young bird should be given the opportunity to learn to fly naturally before it is clipped. An experienced breeder will allow young cockatiels free flight, and the wings will be clipped ready for sale.

MORE THAN ONE?

As flock birds, cockatiels are naturally gregarious. They enjoy each other's company and spend large amounts of time interacting with each other. They "talk" to each other, feed together, and form close bonds with each other.

If you are venturing into cockatiel ownership for the first time, you may well decide that it is better to start off with one bird. Keeping a single bird may suit you—and the space you have available—and you may not wish to have more. If you opt for keeping a single bird, you must be prepared to provide the company, companionship, and stimulation that a cockatiel would derive from living with other birds. This is no hardship. It is wonderful to spend time interacting with a cockatiel, and there is no doubt that your bird will be a great deal tamer than if it lived with other cockatiels.

If you want to keep more than one cockatiel, it is best to start off by buying a single cockatiel, and when it has settled in its new home, you can add another bird. This gives the first cockatiel a chance to bond with you, and you can hand-train it without the distraction of another bird (see Chapter 8). After a couple of months, you can buy a companion for your cockatiel.

MALE OR FEMALE?

Many pet owners prefer cocks, as they are more glamorous than hens and they are more likely to learn to talk. However, hen owners say they are gentle and relate especially well to their owners.

The problem is finding out what sex your cockatiel is. In most color varieties, juveniles look like hens until after their first molt, which occurs at around six months. At that stage, the cocks develop their mature adult coloring. An experienced breeder may be able to sex young birds, but this is not always the case.

Generally, cockatiels are sold at around eight weeks of age, which is when they are old enough to settle into a new home and are ready to adapt to new training regimes. The problem with this is that you may have to leave the question of sex to chance. If you are keeping a single cockatiel, this may not concern you greatly, but it is more of an issue if you plan to keep more than one cockatiel.

If you have a cock and a hen, they will inevitably breed. Breeding is a specialized

The cockatiel's crest tends to be bigger in males (pictured) than in hens.

business (see Chapter 10), and is not a good plan for the first-time owner. Ideally, you will be able to find a same-sex pair (two males or two females). Same-sex pairs will get on just as well as a male and female combination, although obviously there will be no chance of offspring. However, you may well find that one of the cockatiels in a same-sex pair will adopt the role of the absent sex. They will form a strong bond, and may go through the motions of mating and nesting behavior. If you have two hens, they may produce infertile eggs, which can result in health problems (see Egg Binding, page 125). Cockatiels kept in pairs will rarely be as tame as single cockatiels, as they relate more closely with their fellow cockatiels than with their human owner.

DNA TESTING

If you want to be 100 percent sure of a young bird's sex, it will have to be DNA tested (see Chapter 10: Breeding and Exhibiting Cockatiels).

ADOPTING A COCKATIEL

There are rescue sanctuaries for parrots that need rehoming, and there are some that deal specifically with cockatiels. A tiel may need rehoming for a variety of different reasons, and very often the bird is not to blame. In most cases, the previous owner can no longer provide a suitable home, and the bird is simply in need of a new, permanent home. In a few cases, the cockatiel may have been mistreated, and may be suffering from some degree of trauma.

If you want to rescue a cockatiel, think very carefully before you go ahead. A bird that is forced to change homes will need special care to help it to settle, and you will need to devote some time to helping it adapt. If you have some experience keeping cockatiels, you will probably find this task easier.

COCKATIEL COLORS

As we have seen, the wild cockatiel is a predominantly gray bird. If a color mutation occurred in the wild, the bird would probably not survive for long, as it would be easily spotted by predators. But when birds are kept in captivity, breeders can develop new color varieties by using selective breeding programs.

Over the years, new colors and markings have been developed, and a number of varieties are now well established. It is the choice of colors that has, to a large extent, added to the cockatiel's popularity as a pet.

In fact, the cockatiel's color range is limited, as its feather structure lacks the blue layer that is present in parakeets, which results in the huge number of color variations in this species. However, the plumage of a well-marked cockatiel is stunning.

If you are planning to breed cockatiels, color will be a major consideration when you are choosing birds. For pet owners, however, it all comes down to personal preference, as there is no difference between the color varieties.

Normal gray

This is the name given to the cockatiel's traditional wild color. The body is gray, and the outer wing edges are white. The underside of the cock's tail feathers are gray-black; in females and juveniles (before their first molt) the tail feathers are barred with yellow. The beak, feet, and legs are gray, and the eyes are dark brown. The cheeks, throat, and the crest are yellow, and there is a splash of orange on the cheek. The cock will be brighter in color than the hen with more distinct cheek patches.

Lutino

This is the most popular of the cockatiel varieties. It was developed in the late 1950s by a breeder named Mrs. E. L. Moon, who lived in Florida. To begin with, lutino cockatiels, who were also known as "moonbeams" after their breeder, changed hands for vast sums of money. However, the variety is now readily available at low cost. The color of the plumage is white to creamy yellow, with orange cheek patches. Breeders consider the deeper shades (known as "buttercups") to be most desirable. There is also an attractive pearl lutino variety (see below). Lutinos have red eyes, and their beaks and feet are pink.

Lutino hens have bright yellow spots under the flight feathers, and their tails will show a yellow on cream, or cream on yellow, barring pattern. Cocks do not have these traits.

Pearl

The pearl variety was developed in Germany in 1967. On the wings and back, the pattern on the plumage is scalloped, sometimes referred to as "lacewing." Each feather is gray with a yellow edging or yellow edged with gray. The cockatiel's head is yellow, and the tail feathers are barred black and yellow. Hens retain this coloring throughout their lives, but cocks gradually lose the patterning and become a solid color.

In the United States, breeders have been working to establish lines where the cocks do not lose their patterning as they mature.

Nomal gray: The traditional wild color.

Lutino: Different shades are available.

Pearl: Also known as lacewing.

Pied

The pied pattern is the oldest of the cockatiel color varieties. The mutation first appeared in Southern California in 1949, in the aviaries of R. Kersh and D. Putnam. Birds display varying amounts of white, yellow, and gray in their plumage. The patterning can vary dramatically from birds that appear almost normal gray with a few small specks of white, to those that appear almost white and yellow with a few gray areas. Breeders generally try to produce pied where a quarter of the plumage is dark gray and the remainder is clear. Pied cockatiels have dark eyes.

Cinnamon

Established by a Belgian breeder in the late 1960s, this color is sometimes referred to as Isabelle. The plumage has a brownish tinge, which replaces the gray on normal grays and extends to the legs, feet, and eyes. The shade varies between individual birds, but cocks are always darker than hens. After the first molt, the cock acquires a dark, rather than barred, underside to the tail feathers. The cinnamon color can be combined with the pied and the pearl varieties. Cinnamon birds have dark eyes, and their beaks and feet are grayish in color.

Fallow

Developed by a Florida breeder in 1971, this color remains best known in the United States. A fallow cockatiel has red eyes, and its beak and feet are pink. They are paler and more yellow colored than cinnamons, with a grayish yellow body color. Cocks are generally darker.

Albino

The albino cockatiel has no color pigment at all. It has pure white feathers and no cheek patches. It has red eyes, a pink beak, and pink feet. Hens and cocks cannot be visually sexed.

Whiteface

This variety, originally called charcoal, was developed in Europe in the late 1970s. The whiteface cockatiel is a normal gray, with no yellow or orange coloration. Cocks have a distinctive white head; hens have small amounts of white on their faces, and black and white barred tail feathers. More recently, cockatiels have been bred where the orange cheek patches are replaced by yellow, to create a yellow-faced cockatiel.

Silver

This is a recent color mutation, and it was developed in the U.K. in 1980. A breeder in a pet shop spotted a silver-colored cock. The bird's parents were traced, only to find that the cock had died. The breeder therefore bred the mother with the young silvered cock, and produced three silver cocks. A process of selective breeding then established the silver color as a new variety.

The effect of this color mutation is to dilute the normal gray coloring to produce a lighter-colored bird. It comes in two forms: the single factor is more common and the plumage is darker, and the double factor is very light silver in color. Both types have dark eyes, beak, and feet.

Pied: The gray, yellow, and white patterning can vary dramatically.

Whiteface: There is no orange or yellow coloration. This cockatiel is a whiteface pearl pied.

Albino: Pure white feathers with no markings.

Cinnamon: feathers are gray brown, replacing the dark gray on normal grays.

Olive

This is one of the latest colors to be developed, and it is still relatively rare. Olive birds have light gray feathers with a heavy yellow wash, which makes the feather appear greenish.

Olive cockatiels have a slightly scalloped pattern on their wing feathers.

Pastelface

Pastelface cockatiels have a reduced amount of yellow and red in their plumage, which gives their cheek patches a pastel appearance.

Yellowcheek

Also known as yellowface, this type of cockatiel has yellow cheek patches rather than orange.

IN TUNE WITH COCKATIELS

Chris Hardwick of Colorado had no intention of becoming a cockatiel owner until the day came to buy a present for his niece.

"My sister-in-law has a young daughter, Makala, who was about eight years old at the time," says Chris. "A year earlier I had visited a bird show where they had cockatiels for sale. I told my sister-in-law about this and she asked me to buy a cockatiel for Makala. So, when the bird show was next on, my wife and I went along to choose a bird.

"I spotted a breeder who had three young children, all about seven to ten years old, and I could tell that the kids had handled the birds quite a bit because all of them were very tame. The breeder had quite a few birds, including a pearl-pied cockatiel she knew for sure was a male. I bought that one for Makala. But another bird—a bright yellow-pied cockatiel—had also caught my eye. I had never handled a bird before, other than a canary (which can't bite), so I was a bit intimidated by this bird that I was told could really bite hard if it wanted to! But I couldn't help it; I'd never really considered myself a 'bird person' before but I fell in love with that cockatiel and I ended up buying both birds. The breeder told me they were both males.

"When I bought my pet I knew very little about cockatiels, but I learned quite a bit from a lengthy discussion from the breeder, who also gave me a pamphlet that was helpful. To begin with, I handled my new pet with gloves because I was a little nervous about being bitten. But it wasn't long before I was able to take off my gloves. I decided to name my bird B-Flat, because 'he' kept chirping the same note over and over, and to me it sounded like the note

Male cockatiel Bobby quickly mastered the art of talking.

'B-flat'—although I never used a tuner to confirm that! After about six months, I decided to have B-Flat DNA tested, to be absolutely sure 'he' was male. So I plucked a feather—B-Flat didn't like that at all—and sent it off to have it tested. The results came back as 99.99% positive that B-Flat was a male. Then 'he' laid an egg and I knew for sure! I called the DNA-testing company and they refunded me the cost of the test.

"As time passed I became increasingly fond of my 'Little Squeaker' as I had nicknamed her. I tried to take her out of the cage every day and play with her so that she would bond with me, although trying to get her back in her cage could be frustrating sometimes! I found out that Makala had named her bird 'Bobby' and that Bobby went everywhere with Makala, always perched on her shoulder. There were reports that Bobby was actually starting to talk! I tried to get B-Flat to talk for quite some time, but she never said a single word. I loved being able to hold her and play with her, though.

"One day, there was a terrible accident at Makala's. The family's dog went after Bobby and Bobby didn't survive. It was a tragic end to a much-loved bird, and, for many weeks, we all were very sad. I reluctantly decided to give Makala B-Flat as a replacement for Bobby but B-Flat just wasn't the same. She wasn't as affectionate, especially when she laid an egg. After a while, Makala realized that no bird could replace Bobby and she returned B-Flat to me. The prodigal bird had returned! Since then I've become very attached to my Little Squeaker and I love having her around, especially when she begs to come out to sit on my shoulder. I wouldn't be without her now."

Although Chris never wanted a pet cockatiel initially, he has formed a strong attachment to B-Flat.

CHAPTER THREE

PREPARING FOR COCKATIELS

Now that you have decided that the cockatiel is the right bird for you to keep as a pet, and you have located a reputable source for buying birds, you will need to make preparations to turn your home into a cockatiel-friendly environment.

SETTING UP A HOME

In the wild, cockatiels spend most of their time on the wing. They are fast and agile, and are among the best fliers of the Parrot family. Cockatiels have adapted well to living in captivity, but it is important to provide as much space as possible.

When cockatiels and other members of the Parrot family (such as parakeets) were first kept as pets, it was considered perfectly reasonable to confine birds in small cages for long periods every day. Birds were rarely allowed out of their cages, and it says a lot for the hardiness of cockatiels and parakeets that they managed to

cope with such an unstimulating lifestyle. Fortunately, we now have a far greater understanding of what pet birds need, and, with careful thought and planning, we can provide a home where captive birds will thrive.

AN INDOOR HOME

Cockatiels are such lively, sociable birds that they enjoy living in an indoor home, interacting with members of the family and observing the comings and goings of a busy household.

The cage

If you are keeping cockatiels in your home, they will need to be caged, but this no longer means a life sentence of misery for the captive bird. Cages have been revolutionized so birds have the space to fly from perch to perch. When you are choosing a cage, you will need to consider the following points:

You do not have to spend vast amounts of money on a flashy cage, but if you buy the largest you can afford, your cockatiels will be much happier.

- Size: Buy the biggest cage you can afford. The minimum size for two cockatiels is 23 inches (58 cm) tall, 18 inches (46 cm) deep, and 30 inches (76 cm) long, but your birds will be much happier if they have more space.
- Shape: The best cage shape is rectangular or square.
- Bars: The space between bars should be no more than 0.75 inch (19 mm). Horizontal bars are recommended, as they give the cockatiels an opportunity to climb.
- Sliding tray: This will allow you to change the floor covering easily.
- Secure door: The door should be large enough for easy cleaning and handling. It must be fitted with a secure fastening.

Placing the cage

Cockatiels want to be part of the family, so do not put the cage in a room that is rarely used. However, you need to be aware of household hazards that could pose a danger to your birds. When you are deciding where to position the cage, weigh the following considerations:

- The cage should be in a light, airy position, which is free from drafts. A corner position is ideal.
- Make sure the cage is not in direct sunlight for lengthy periods, or your cockatiels will become overheated. For the same reason, do not put the cage close to a radiator.
- If the cage does not come with a stand, you will need a strong, secure base.
- The cage should be positioned just below your eye level, so you can talk to your bird.
- If you have other pets, such as a cat or a dog, the cage must be out of their reach.
- Check that your cockatiel cannot reach out of the cage to get at electric wires or at curtains, which will be shredded in no time.
- Avoid the kitchen, where your tiel could be exposed to toxic fumes.

FIXTURES AND FITTINGS

In both a cage and an aviary, there are a variety of furnishings you will need for your birds' home.

Perches

A cage may come equipped with perches, but they may not be suitable for cockatiels. A cockatiel needs perches that range in diameter between ⅜ to ¾ inch (9.5 mm and 19 mm) so that its toes fit around 50–75 percent of the circumference of the perch. The reason for this is to protect the bird's feet. If a cockatiel always lands on a perch of the same diameter, it will always be using the same part of its foot. In time, the cockatiel will develop sores or hardened skin. The solution is to provide a variety of perches so a cockatiel can fully exercise its toes and nails. The best perches are natural wood, which cockatiels enjoy gnawing.

AN OUTDOOR AVIARY

Most cockatiel breeders will have an aviary, which will be an attractive feature of the garden, as well as providing a home for multiple birds. If you have an aviary, you can also consider keeping a number of different species of birds. Cockatiels are sociable birds and will live happily with many of the smaller Australian and Asian parakeets. They get on particularly well with parakeets, as they both come from the Australian outback and share a similar lifestyle.

There are a number of factors to consider before building an aviary.

• Climate: The cockatiel originates from the Australian outback and its body is geared to living in a hot, dry climate. Captive-bred cockatiels will adapt to different temperatures, but they cannot stand extreme cold. If you want to set up an aviary, you need to live in a region that has a temperate climate.

• Space: Do you have enough room in your garden to build an aviary? Most aviaries are composed of a large outdoor flight, and an indoor shelter where the birds can roost.

Continued on page 30

If you have the space, you can buy a metal, ready-made aviary.

AN OUTDOOR AVIARY

Continued from page 29

- Noise: Do you live close to other houses? Avian enthusiasts enjoy the sounds that their birds make, but your neighbors may not be so appreciative.
- Planning permission: You will need to check local regulations to see if you need permission to build an outside aviary.
- Cost: A specially built aviary requires considerable financial investment.

Before you decide that an aviary is the ideal way to keep cockatiels, consider the sort of relationship you want with your birds. Aviary birds relate to each other, and although they can be trained so they are happy to be handled, they will never be as tame as cockatiels that are kept in the home.

PLACING AN AVIARY

If you are ready to go ahead with building an aviary, you will need to decide where to place it. Consider what is best for your cockatiels and what is most convenient for you:

- The land should be as level as possible. If you need to use sloping land, check out the drainage. You need to avoid land that becomes waterlogged after rain.
- Try to find a site that is not too exposed to cold winds or is subject to hours of sunshine.
- The aviary should be located away from trees and overhanging branches, which create a damp environment after rainfall, encouraging the growth of fungus. You will also have problems in the fall when leaves are falling. Rodents are very clever at using overhanging branches as a way of gaining access to the roof of the aviary.
- Ideally, you want to place the aviary where you can view it from the house.
- It is advisable to avoid a site where the aviary can be seen from the road. Unfortunately, thefts from aviaries are not unknown.

BASIC CONSTRUCTION

The beauty of an aviary is that you can design it to your own specifications. Depending on the space you have available, you can work out the size, materials, and whether you are able to connect it with water and electricity supplies. This is by no means essential, but it certainly makes routine maintenance a lot easier. Aviaries are timber-framed, or you can buy ready-made metal aviaries.

Most aviaries have three basic units:

The base: This is the floor of the aviary, and it should extend beyond the perimeter of the aviary complex. The base should slope gently away from the aviary buildings to allow for easy cleaning. The base should be made of concrete, slabs, or gravel. A grass or bare earth surface is not suitable, as it cannot be cleaned properly.

The flight: This is the area allocated for free flight. Make this space as long as possible for fast-flying cockatiels. The minimum length is 6 feet (1.8 m); this is also the minimum for height. The flight is composed of a weld mesh gauge, which should have a thickness of 16–19 g (1.6–1 mm). The hole size should be 1 x 1 inch (2.5 x 2.5 cm), which will prevent rodents and wild birds from gaining entry. The wire is likely to contain zinc, which is a potential risk. Wire should be of a good quality and must be electro galvanized rather than dip galvanized. In the latter case, droplets of metal tend to be left on the wire, which birds take great pleasure in biting off and swallowing, rapidly leading to poisoning and likely death, if not treated very soon by an experienced bird veterinarian.

It is a good idea to cover part of the flight with opaque plastic roofing sheets so your cockatiels can shelter from the rain. If you are planning to use the flight as your point of entry, you need to build a safety porch, so you can close a door

An aviary is the best solution if you are keeping a large number of birds.

behind you before going into the flight.

The flight should be furnished with a variety of perches (see pages 28 and 32), plus food and water dishes (see page 33).

The shelter: This is an enclosed room, which leads on from the flight. It should be well insulated, frost-free, well lit, and equipped with perches and feeding platforms. This is the place where your cockatiels will come in to feed, where they will roost at night, and where they will find protection from the weather. If you have room, you can add a bird room alongside the shelter, which you can use for storing food and equipment.

Ideally, a cockatiel should have natural wood perches of varying diameters.

Select branches of varying diameters, and cut them to the right size for your cage or aviary. Always avoid plastic perches, as they will result in sores on the underneath of the toes and the feet.

Before you position the perches, wash them thoroughly to remove any traces of chemical spray or contamination from wild birds. A cage for two cockatiels needs two or three perches. It is better not to overcrowd the cage, so the birds have maximum flying room.

If you have an aviary, the perches should be located at different heights, at either end of the flight. Again, this gives the maximum flying space.

SAFE WOOD TO USE FOR PERCHES

Apple	Citrus (orange, lemon)	Guava	Maple
Ash		Hawthorn	Pine
Aspen	Elm	Hazelnut	Poplar
Beech	Eucalyptus	Larch	Sycamore
Birch	Fir	Manzanita	Willow

Unsafe woods include: acaia, chestnut, dogwood, laurel, laburnum, those belonging to the Prunus family (such as apricot, cherry, and peach), and yew.

Branches with a rough contour and of such a diameter that a cockatiel's toes fit around 50–75 percent of the circumference of the branch are ideal. The best branches are fruit trees (so long as they have not been sprayed with any insecticide), willow, birch, maple, oak, lime, walnut, and hazelnut. It is essential to avoid acacia, chestnut, dogwood, laurel, laburnum, and yew trees.

Nest provision

A nestbox should not be provided unless you have a mixed-sex pair and you actively want to breed them (see Chapter 10). In other situations it will stimulate breeding, which will then be nonproductive and will be frustrating for the poor birds.

Base-lining material

An aviary will have a concrete or gravel floor, but if you have a cage, you will need to provide a lining for the base. Like all members of the Parrot family, cockatiels are messy birds and are happy to scatter their food as they search for the tastiest morsels. Water may get spilled, and the base will also become dirty with droppings. A bird keeper must keep the cage clean and hygienic, so it is important to find a base-lining material that is easy to replace on a routine basis. Bird keepers have experimented with different materials, and some have proved more successful than others.

- **Pine shavings:** This material looks attractive, but is has to be changed frequently to avoid the buildup of bacteria.
- **Sandpaper:** You can buy sheets of sandpaper to line the base of your cage, but this can result in sore feet.
- **Newspaper:** This is the preferred choice, particularly in the U.K. It is readily available, cheap, easy to change—and cockatiels also enjoy shredding it!
- **Corncob bedding:** This is a popular choice in the United States. It is dust-free, traps odors,

and is highly absorbent. It should be changed regularly to avoid the possibility of mold.

Never use cat litter to line the base of the cage. A cockatiel could ingest this type of material, which would be highly dangerous.

Food and water dishes

You will need dishes for water, seed, and fruit and vegetables. You can buy dishes made of plastic, stainless steel, or pottery. Some types can be clipped to the side of the cage; others are freestanding. Cockatiels are not as destructive as some members of the Parrot family that are kept as pets, so you can choose plastic dishes. However, they can be more easily tipped over than pottery or stainless steel dishes. Many bird keepers prefer stainless steel dishes, as they are durable and easy to clean.

You can provide water in a gravity-fed water bottle attached to the bars of the cage. Some tiels are very happy with this arrangement, while others are reluctant to drink from a bottle. If you

Bowls can be clipped to the side of the cage to help avoid spillage.

want to try a bottle, make sure your cockatiels are using it before you remove the water dish.

If you are keeping more than one cockatiel, it is a good plan to place a couple of food dishes at either end of the cage or aviary. This ensures that all cockatiels get an equal share of the food, as, in some situations, a more dominant bird may try to monopolize the tastiest food. If you have an aviary, make sure that food and water dishes are located in places where they remain dry; do not place dishes underneath perches where the food will become contaminated with droppings.

Bath

Cockatiels love to bathe, and they need access to water in order to keep their feathers in good shape (see page 62). If you have a reasonably large cage, you can attach a bath to the cage door. These are particularly useful in hot weather and when a cockatiel is molting (see page 63). In an aviary, you can provide a large, shallow earthenware dish and fill it with water to a depth of approximately one inch (2.5 cm). If you want to go for special effects, you can buy a bird bath that has a built-in waterfall. This looks attractive and is greatly appreciated by cockatiels.

Toys

Cockatiels are intelligent birds that thrive on activity and mental stimulation. Providing toys is therefore an important part of caring for your bird, particularly if it is living in a cage. Aviary birds have more opportunity for natural activity and exercise, and are not so dependent on playthings.

If you visit a store that specializes in birds and bird equipment, you will be amazed at the choice of toys that is available. It is important to consider the natural behavior of your birds when you are choosing toys, so that you buy playthings that are most beneficial.

TOYS FOR COCKATIELS

Wooden blocks are ideal for gnawing.

A bell can be used as a training toy.

Make sure there is sufficient space when you add a swing.

- **Gnawing toys:** Cockatiels like to gnaw; this is a cockatiel's way of investigating a new object, and it also helps to keep the beak trim (see page 66). The best toys for cockatiels are wooden blocks and lengths of rope threaded with wooden blocks or knotted leather thongs. Tiels are attracted by bright objects, so you can indulge in toys in a variety of different colors.

  The tough, plastic rings used for teething babies provide good gnawing material for cockatiels. Avoid cheap plastic toys, such as those that are often sold as parakeet toys, as these can splinter and cause injury. Rubber can be poisonous to cockatiels if swallowed, so avoid toys made of this material.

  Gnawing toys do not have to cost money. For example, cockatiels enjoy pecking softwood branches (the type that make suitable perches, see page 32).
- **Food toys:** There are some toys that incorporate food, such as maize, for the birds to peck at. You can hang this type of toy up in the cage, and your cockatiels will love it. You can also hang a bunch of green food (see page 56) from the bars of the cage, or attach a cuttlefish bone (see page 57). This has the double bonus of providing food and activity for your cockatiels. Cockatiels enjoy playing with pinecones. Hide some food treats in the cones so your tiels will get a tasty surprise.
- **Gymnastic toys:** Cockatiels are great climbers and acrobats, so sturdy ladders and climbing platforms will be appreciated. They will also enjoy playing on swings and hoops.

CRAMPED FOR SPACE

Beware of filling the cage with too many toys. The top priority is to provide the maximum space for your cockatiel to fly. If the cage is littered with toys, the bird will be cramped, and will also become bored with its toys. Most bird keepers adopt a system of rotating toys, one or two at a time. This keeps the cage uncluttered, and the toys will retain their novelty value.

- **Training toys:** Teach your cockatiels to perform tricks, such as ringing a bell (see page 88). Tiels are quick to learn and enjoy performing this type of trick, but you may find the noise gets a little trying after a while!
- **Shredding toys:** Cockatiels enjoy shredding material and will have great fun ripping up an old paperback book or a cardboard tube. You will have to clear up the debris, but it is worth the effort to keep your cockatiels entertained.

Night-light

In common with other members of the Parrot family, cockatiels can suffer from "night frights" (see page 102). This is when a bird is startled at night, and crashes around the cage or aviary in a panic. A night-light, with a low wattage (8–25 watts) reduces the risk of night frights, as the birds are not in complete darkness and are less likely to be startled.

You need to ensure that you provide a safe environment when your cockatiel is allowed out of the cage.

OUTSIDE THE CAGE

The cage should be seen as your cockatiel's home base, where it roosts at night, where it feeds, and where it spends some periods of the day. However, your cockatiel should also be allowed extended periods of time outside its cage. Your cockatiel will enjoy the chance to come out of its cage and explore a wider environment, but it is vital that you provide a safe environment for it. In most cases, you will release your cockatiels in the room where the cage is located. Before you attempt to do this, you must ensure that your cockatiels cannot get into any dangerous situations. If your cockatiel has had its wings clipped, it will have restricted flight, but there are still many potential hazards awaiting the curious cockatiel

COCKATIELS BEWARE!

If your cockatiel is flighted, there are many dangers that you should be aware of. Tragically, many cockatiels are lost or die as a result of spending time outside their cage in an environment that has not been checked for safety. The most common dangers a free-flying cockatiel is exposed to include the following:

- Escape or loss of the bird when someone leaves the window open or opens a door.
- Attack by another pet (such as a cat).
- Landing in a fire/cooking pan.
- Impact with a rotating ceiling fan.

- Eating or drinking toxic compounds, such as chocolate, coffee, avocado.
- Being caught in a door as someone is trying to close it.
- Toxic fumes (see teflon toxicity, page 126), plus any aerosols, overheated cooking fat, cement dust, any smoke (including cigarettes), any other noxious fumes.
- Lead poisoning (such as lead strips in windows or doors, antique ornaments, fishing weights, old paintings, wood carvings, galvanized wire, old glazed ceramics, wheel balancers, lightbulb base, linoleum and

To make a room safe for cockatiels, you must take the following measures:

- Check out all possible escape routes, ensuring that windows and doors are closed. If possible, screen the windows with net curtains, as your cockatiel may attempt to fly straight through the glass.
- Fit a few perches around the room, so your cockatiel has places to land, and it will be easier for you to keep a check on its whereabouts.
- If you have an open fire, or an electric fire, make sure you have a suitable fireguard to prevent possible injury. If you have an unused fireplace, it will also need to be shielded to prevent escapes up the chimney.

- Electric wires pose a major danger to a cockatiel, as it cannot resist gnawing them. You will need to devise a system to clean up all trailing wires.

Playstand

When your cockatiel is out of its cage, it will need a base where it can perch, feed, and drink. Avian stores have a range of playstands, which are ideal for this purpose. Some are free-standing, and, for smaller birds such as cockatiels, you can get a stand that can be put on a tabletop. The playstand can be very simple, or it may come equipped with a variety of perches, swings, ladders, and toys. All types of playstands come with a tray, which is placed beneath the stand to catch droppings.

---

roofing felt, certain lubricants, old plaster, putty, costume jewelry, lead- or glass-stained windows, seeds for planting, wine bottle tops, horticultural grade plastics, polythene or PVC, curtain weights, etc.)

- Zinc poisoning, such as galvanized wire, clips, padlocks, and feeding bowls especially when new, white rust on older galvanized products, metallic game pieces and other toys, any nonstainless steel metallic objects, some coins (especially foreign), wire or C clips used to attach food or toys in the cage, bone substitutes on cutlery handles, dental cement,

cellulose lacquers, germicidal products, medical bandages, shaving cream, soap, lotions and cosmetics, enamel and stove finishes, fire-proofed fabrics, glazes on porcelain, greases and lubricants, linoleum and oil cloths, chemical agent in rayons, paints, plastics, printing inks, rubber, sneakers and rubber shoes, waterproofing of paper, leather, and textiles, weighting agent for silks, wood preservatives.

For information on preparing your cockatiel for time outside its cage, see page 48 and Chapter 8

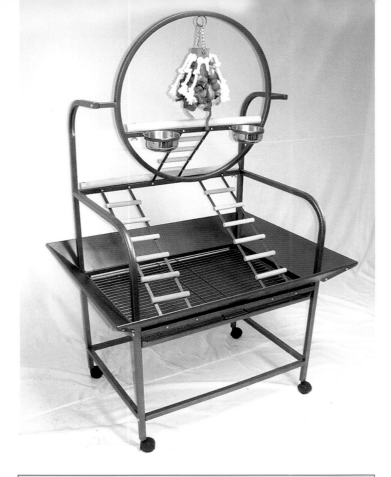

A playstand will give your cockatiel a base when it is outside the cage.

FINDING A VETERINARIAN

Once you have bought all the equipment you need, and have prepared a home for your cockatiel, you are nearly ready to go out and choose a bird. But there is one more important task. If you are keeping a pet, you are responsible for all its needs—and that includes health care. Obviously, you hope the cockatiel you buy will be fit and well, and, with good care, it should suffer few serious problems. However, before you bring your tiel home, you should track down a veterinarian who specializes in birds. You will need expert veterinary advice when you are planning routine preventive health care. You may need to seek help with nail or beak trimming, and there may be times when your cockatiel is unwell and you need to call in a veterinarian.

Some small animal practices treat birds along with dogs, cats, and other small animals. Ideally, you want at least one veterinarian in the practice who is a specialized avian veterinarian. Birds are not easy to treat. It is essential to find a veterinarian who has experience with birds, and with cockatiels in particular.

TIEL TIP

To contact an avian veterinarian in your area, get in touch with:

USA
Association of Avian Veterinarians
P.O. Box 811720
Boca Raton, FL 33481
http://www.aav.org/

UK
The National Council for Aviculture
4 Haven Crescent
Werrington, Stoke-on-Trent
Staffordshire, ST9 OEY

HOME FROM HOME

Maureen Cranston of Northumberland, England, has been keeping cockatiels for more than 15 years—and now she has an aviary full of cockatiels that is her pride and joy.

"It all started with a single bird in a cage and just grew from there," says Maureen. "Cockatiels are addictive birds because they are so entertaining. Needless to say, one bird became many because I loved the variety of colors, and I soon came to believe that they should be kept in a flock."

Initially, Maureen kept her cockatiels in a cage, but, as her feathered family grew and she got to know more about her pets and their needs, she decided to build them an aviary. "I love birds but I like to see them

Maureen wanted to give her cockatiels more freedom than a cage could provide, and so she constructed an aviary.

with space to fly around freely and enjoy the outdoors. Carrying the cage outside in the summer wasn't really enough, so I built my very first flight around 13 years ago. It was done in a hurry and with no expert advice. It was a poor first effort with its roof entirely undercover, a soil floor, and wire mesh that was large and clumsy. I've learned a lot since then.

"The most important point to remember is that the aviary should be placed where you want it, and not where you think it will fit. By making your own aviary you can adapt it to fit the shape and space available. All my aviaries are built on the principle of an indoor roosting area and an outdoor flight. The flight should be as large as possible, bearing in mind that length is more important than height for flying birds. My aviary has a roosting area of three feet by six feet, and a flight area of six feet by twelve feet. The flight is sheltered, with part of the roof covered to allow my birds a bit of protection from the elements.

"When you construct an aviary, you need to give a surprising amount of thought to the floor. Cockatiels can make a real mess! My aviary has a concrete floor with drain holes down the sides, so that I can hose it down daily.

Continued on page 40

HOME FROM HOME

Continued from page 39

"Predators are another concern. I feed my birds in the indoor area of their aviary, to deter rodents from coming for food. To make an aviary rodent-proof and to protect the birds from cats and birds of prey, the flight may need to be double-netted. I've found an air staple gun to be an invaluable weapon for making the aviary secure, and it saves the fingers!

"It's really important to me that my birds have a good life, as close as possible to their natural habitat, so I've spent a lot of time 'accessorizing' my aviary. I put in fresh branches regularly, although they are destroyed very rapidly! I try to use as many natural branches as possible in the flights, to prove good exercise for the birds' feet and a more natural feel underfoot.

"I love having an outdoor aviary. I feel that the birds are being kept far more naturally and with a great deal more freedom than those in a cage. Bird keeping is a really enjoyable hobby and you get to observe the birds and their behavior when you have a flock living in an aviary. One of my favorite moments is the routine spraying of the birds. Because there are quite a few, I use a hosepipe attachment set on spray. To see the birds all hanging upside down with their wings out, enjoying their shower, is the most hilarious sight I have ever seen. Mind

Maureen has learned a lot about aviary construction over the years, and is now able to provide an ideal environment for her flock.

you, the first time for the young is usually like a kid with a bath—not appreciated!

"If you own several cockatiels, I'd definitely recommend thinking about building an aviary. But before doing anything, consider your neighbors. Cockatiels are noisy birds, and your neighbors will not be happy if your aviary is right under their bedroom! If you can find a suitable place in your garden, though, there are definite advantages to keeping cockatiels in an aviary instead of a cage. It is closer to the birds' natural environment, it's an ideal solution for people who suffer from allergies and cannot keep a pet in the house, for house-proud bird lovers it saves a great deal of mess in the house, and, most importantly of all, the birds love it!"

CHAPTER FOUR

ARRIVING HOME

O nce you have set up a suitable cockatiel home, you are ready to go out and buy a bird. Resist the temptation of trying to purchase a cockatiel and equipment on the same day. You need time to get yourself properly organized before you have a living creature to care for.

As discussed previously, if you are planning to keep more than one cockatiel, it is better to start off buying one tiel and then adding a companion bird once the first cockatiel has settled. If possible, ask an experienced bird keeper to come with you when you are making your first purchase. It is all too easy for your heart to rule your head, so avoid the risk by enlisting the help of an objective expert.

TRANSPORT

When you have selected a cockatiel, having picked out your preferred color and ensured that it is a young bird around two months of age, you will need to transport it home. Avian stores sell specially made bird carriers that are lightweight and made of cardboard. This type is inexpensive and is often flat-packed so you can assemble it at the store. There is nothing wrong with this type of carrier, but you should bear in mind that it is suitable for only a short trip and will not last very long.

It is advisable to buy a more substantial carrier made of plastic or wood. This type of carrier is usually fitted with a perch and a front wire grill, which allows for light and ventilation. Although it costs more, this is an investment you will not regret. If a bird becomes sick, you can take it to the veterinarian without delay. The carrier will also prove useful for routine visits to the veterinarian for bill clipping, etc. (see Chapter 6). If you are going on vacation, and you have arranged for another bird keeper to care for your cockatiels, you will be able to transport the birds in complete safety, and then set up the cage when you arrive at your destination.

If you are traveling by car, place the carrier in the coolest part of the vehicle where there is no danger of it toppling over. The space behind the front seats is safe and secure. Do not put the carrier in the trunk, as there is a danger that deadly fumes from the exhaust could leak in. If your trip is relatively short (no more than a couple of hours), you do not need to worry about feeding your cockatiel or providing drinking water. The bird will probably be too stressed to feed when it is traveling, so wait until you arrive home before offering nourishment.

INTO THE CAGE

If you are starting off with a single bird, you can simply transfer your cockatiel from its carrier to the cage. At this stage, it is important to consider the upheaval involved in changing homes. A young cockatiel is only just beginning to learn about the world, and suddenly everything that is familiar vanishes. Fortunately, cockatiels are outgoing and inquisitive, and your bird will soon adapt to its new surroundings. But for the first few days, it is kinder to keep noise levels low, and allow the tiel to look out on its new surroundings with the minimum of disturbance. Obviously you will be changing food and water bowls, so the bird will start to become familiar with you. Do not attempt to touch the cockatiel, or worse still, try to grab it. The cockatiel will become fearful every time it sees your hand, and will be impossible to tame. The best plan is to come up to the cage, and talk to your young cockatiel. The bird will learn to recognize your voice and will begin to bond with you.

QUARANTINE

If you are introducing a new cockatiel to an existing setup, you will need to keep the newcomer in quarantine. There are fatal diseases, viruses, and bacterial infections that can be transmitted through the air, so you will need to keep a new bird in a separate cage, in a different room to begin with. A cockatiel may appear to be perfectly healthy, but it could be suffering from an underlying disease that could be triggered with the stress of moving to a new home. To be safe, you should keep a new bird in quarantine for a minimum of 30 days. Check regularly to ensure that the tiel is eating well, has normal droppings, and is taking a lively interest in its surroundings. If you have any concern about the cockatiel's state of health, seek advice from an avian veterinarian.

When the quarantine period is over, you can start to introduce the new bird to your existing setup. To start with, place the newcomer in its

HOT SPOTS

Cockatiels, along with other birds, are very susceptible to heatstroke. The temperature in a car can rise very quickly, so make sure your cockatiel is kept as cool as possible when you are traveling. If you need to stop, do not leave the bird unattended in the car for an extended period.

cage so that it can see your resident cockatiel. After a few weeks, move the cages closer, so the cockatiels can get to know each other. If the birds appear calm and friendly toward each other, you can take both birds out of their cages and allow them to meet each other. Over the next few weeks, you can increase the time spent outside the cage so that the two cockatiels have a chance to bond with each other. When you are confident that the two tiels are getting along, they can be moved into the same cage.

Avoid changes in diet when your cockatiel first arrives home.

CHANGES IN DIET

For the first few days, it is advisable to provide the same type of food (seed or pellet) that the cockatiel was getting at the pet store or with its breeder (see Chapter 5). In fact, if the bird is thriving, there is no need to make changes unless you have problems with availability. However, you will want to add variety to your cockatiel's diet by introducing fresh food. The best plan is to wait a few days until the cockatiel has had a chance to settle. Moving homes is a stressful time for cockatiels and you want to keep changes to a minimum.

If your cockatiel is eating well, and appears bright and lively, you can start introducing new food, such as different types of fruit and vegetables, within a week or so. However, do not challenge your cockatiel's digestive system by giving it lots of different food. Try giving a little of one new type of food to begin with, making sure this does not result in any digestive upsets before trying a new food.

For more information on feeding cockatiels, see Chapter 5: Healthy Eating.

MEETING THE FAMILY

It is an exciting time when a new pet arrives in a household, and, naturally, everyone in the family will want to get to know the new cockatiel. Again, you must consider the tiel's feelings first. Let the bird get used to its new surroundings, and give it a chance to settle. It is very easy to overwhelm a young bird by crowding around its cage—even if you are only gathered to admire the newcomer.

In time, a cockatiel will form a relationship with all members of the family.

If you have children, you must make sure that all visits to the cage are supervised. A cockatiel is not a nervous bird, but it will be startled by sudden movements or loud noises. Generally, children need to be over the age of eight before they can be involved in looking after captive birds. It is not easy for younger children to be sufficiently calm or careful to handle small birds.

When your cockatiel becomes more relaxed, it will learn to recognize all members of the family, and will give a greeting when anyone approaches the cage.

Cats and dogs

Both cats and dogs are natural hunters, and, despite thousands of years of domestication, these instincts remain very strong. Realistically, you cannot expect birds to mix with other pets; the best policy is to avoid confrontations.

If you have a cat, you should keep it well away from your cockatiel at all times. Never let the cat wander unsupervised into the room where your cockatiel is caged. This is simply asking for trouble. If you are in the same room, watching television for example, the cat can be allowed its place on your lap—as long as it is never left alone with a bird.

If you have a dog, you can take steps to train it to ignore your cockatiel.

- Start by arming yourself with treats, and put the dog on the lead.
- Walk toward the cage, making sure the dog remains calm. Allow the dog to stand by the cage and watch the cockatiel.
- Call your dog's name, and the moment the dog switches its attention from the bird to you, reward with a treat and lots of praise. Keep repeating this so that your dog learns that it is more rewarding to focus on you rather than the cockatiel.

- The next step is to allow the dog off lead when the cockatiel is in its cage. Again, keep calling the dog to you and giving rewards. The dog will find you much more interesting than watching a bird, and will soon learn that the cage is of little interest.

In time, you will be able to trust the dog to be in the same room as the cockatiel and take no notice of it. However, you should never allow your dog to be left alone in a room with caged birds. You may be 99 per cent certain that the dog will behave – but it is not worth taking even the smallest risk.

Obviously, dog and cats should never be allowed in the room when the cockatiel is flying free.

JUST ONE MORE...

Liz Crawshay of Bristol, UK, considered her family to be complete, but then she was asked to do a favour for a friend...

"You'd think that two cats and two dogs would be enough for anyone, but I was approached by a friend of my neighbour who was emigrating and had to rehome her pet cockatiel. Knowing that I was an animal lover, she wondered if I'd consider taking on Midge. I'd never had anything to do with pet birds up to that point, and my first instinct was to say no, but I made the mistake of agreeing to see the bird and that was that.

"Midge was quite a tame bird and when I went to meet him he was not in a cage, as I expected, but flying around the living room. His owner, Ruth, called him over and he amazed me by doing just that. I thought only dogs came when called. Midge then startled me even more by introducing himself and saying "Hi, I'm Midge". I've since found out that he doesn't say very much else, but at the time I was really impressed! Midge then hopped from Ruth's finger on to my shoulder and stayed there for the full half an hour that Ruth and I discussed his future. Occasionally, he'd whistle, making his own contribution to the conversation.

"By the end of the visit I was smitten, although I had several concerns – not least my cats. Ruth and her family were not leaving for another six months, so I agreed to take Midge on a trial basis. A week later, Midge came home with me.

"Midge was used to a couple of hours out of his cage each and every day, and I was determined to stick to that routine. The dogs and cats sleep in the kitchen and utility room, so I decided that the living room would be Midge's base. I went round and removed anything that could be hazardous to him and then found him a nice spot for his cage and his play stand. For the first few days, no other animals were allowed in the living room, and then we introduced them very slowly. First the dogs, whom we rewarded with dog treats every time they ignored Midge and concentrated on us instead. Then—my biggest misgiving—we brought in the cats.

"Introducing the cats was planned very carefully. A friend of mine owns a rabbit and has a large outdoor run. I borrowed this and put the cats inside with some toys and food. That way, they could see Midge, they had plenty of room to move around, and plenty to keep them occupied. For the first five minutes both cats quickly ate all the food in the run. For the next five minutes they just stared at Midge's cage, practically salivating at the mouth. After that, they began grooming and playing and ignored him. 'So far, so good,' I thought. I repeated the exercise every day until the cats were totally ignoring Midge. Then I let the cats in the room without using a run. My older cat, Sam, behaved as though Midge didn't exist. To this day, he has hardly shown any interest in Midge. My younger cat, Zoe, was another matter. She went straight over to the cage, sat down in front of it and stared at Midge. Midge didn't seem overly concerned, so I didn't shoo her away. I was expecting this and had come prepared with scraps of ham in my pocket. Once I got them out, Zoe suddenly forgot that there was a potential meal in the cage and remembered that her owner's lap was her favorite place to be.

"I'm still very careful. Whenever Midge comes out of his cage I have to check that there are no cats hiding behind the sofa. You can't fight instinct, and an uncaged bird flying around might prove too much temptation for a hungry cat. I

never allow Midge out of his cage with the cats in the room.

"The dogs are a different story. They usually ignore Midge and have accepted that they are not allowed to hurt him. Midge will land on Labrador Sadie's head occasionally to spend a couple of minutes seeing the world from a dog's perspective. But I never allow the dogs and Midge in the same room together unless I am there to supervise.

"Needless to say, Midge did not go back to Ruth. He's been settled with my husband and me for three years now, and he is definitely one of the family. For someone who never thought of themselves as a 'bird person,' I must admit to being a complete convert."

Cockatiel Midge likes to see the world from a canine perspective.

HANDLING COCKATIELS

If you have bought a cockatiel that has been hand-reared, it should be tame and used to interacting with people. When you have given the bird a chance to settle in its new home, you can start making friends.

The cockatiel you have bought may be used to perching on a finger and being carried from the cage already. But it is advisable to train a new arrival step by step, so that it will learn to trust you and build a relationship with you.

- The cockatiel will be used to your hand taking feeding dishes in and out of the cage and replacing the water dish. Now you can progress to offering your cockatiel a treat, such as a piece of apple or a carrot stick. Do

A cockatiel must learn that there is nothing to fear when you put your hand into its cage.

not make sudden movements, and allow the tiel to approach in its own time.

- It may help if you hold your hand near a perch so the cockatiel can hop onto it and investigate what is going on. It may take a little time and patience, but eventually the curious cockatiel will approach to find out what you are holding. Keep your hand very still, and talk quietly to reassure your cockatiel. Within a few moments of approaching, the cockatiel will usually start to nibble the treat you are holding.
- Repeat this exercise over a few days until your tiel is approaching you confidently to get its treat.
- The next step is to encourage the cockatiel to hop onto the back of your hand or onto your outstretched index finger. You can do this by gently stroking the cockatiel on its chest while it is eating. To begin with, the cockatiel may step back, but it will soon accept the attention. Then stroke gently upward. This will cause the bird either to flutter away or to step onto your hand or finger. Be patient and keep trying until the tiel is happy to use your hand as a perch.
- When the cockatiel is stepping onto your outstretched hand or finger, you can introduce a command, such as "*Up.*"
- If the cockatiel is still wary of your hand, you can try offering a perch. This can be a small branch, a piece of doweling, or it could even be a pencil. Some birds find an inanimate object less scary in the early stages of training. It is a relatively easy matter to coax the tiel to

perch on your hand when it has overcome its initial reluctance.

- When your cockatiel is happy to use your hand as a perch, you need to train it to hop back onto its former perch. This will be particularly important when you are returning a bird to its cage after a period outside its cage (see page 84). Obviously this is much easier, as the cockatiel is returning to something familiar rather than plucking up the courage to hop onto your hand. Position your hand alongside a perch and the tiel will probably step straight onto it. If necessary, place your finger just behind the bird's feet, which will encourage it to move forward. Reward your cockatiel when it is back on the perch. When the cockatiel understands what you want, you can add a word of command, such as *"Down."*
- Only when your cockatiel is completely confident about stepping onto your hand should you attempt to take the bird out of the cage. To begin with, the cockatiel may be worried and fly back to the safety of its cage. But tiels love to explore, and soon it will stay on your hand so it can take a look around the world outside its cage.

NO FEARS

Your aim is to increase the bird's trust and confidence so that you can build up a close and rewarding relationship. The cockatiel should recognize you as leader and accept all procedures without protest. This is not only a sign of trust; it is essential when you are caring for birds. If a bird will not accept routine

A tame cockatiel will be happy to step onto your hand and be carried from the cage.

procedures, such as nail clipping, you will have major problems regarding your cockatiel's health and well-being.

The best way to tame your tiel is to set aside time every day to handle the bird. In the early stages, the cockatiel may do no more than step onto your hand. But with time and patience, the cockatiel will want to spend time with you and will enjoy being petted. Cockatiels like being stroked on their chest. To begin with, a tiel will be wary about being touched behind its head, as it cannot see what is happening, but, in time, cockatiels love this attention. Most cockatiels dislike being stroked along their back, but a cockatiel that is very tame will accept all-over handling, knowing there is nothing to fear.

For more information on training cockatiels, see Chapter 8: Training Cockatiels.

CHAPTER FIVE

HEALTHY EATING

A pet cockatiel is entirely dependent on its keeper for all the food it receives, and therefore this task should be taken very seriously. Like all birds, the cockatiel needs a balanced diet that contains all the nutrients, vitamins, and essential elements necessary for a healthy life. Cockatiels enjoy their food, and a varied diet with occasional treats will make everyday life more rewarding.

In the wild, cockatiels eat seed as their main source of food, along with some plants, fruits, and berries. When we are feeding captive birds, we need to replicate the "wild diet" as closely as possible, as the bird's digestive system is designed to cope with this type of food.

EATING AND DIGESTING

The cockatiel uses its beak to collect seed, and then its thick, fleshy tongue manipulates the seed so it is in the perfect position for cracking and dehusking. It is important to remember that cockatiels discard the seed husks, and these will need to be removed from the feeding area every day. Sadly, there have been too many incidents of pets starving, due to inexperienced bird keepers mistaking the empty seed husks for food.

Once the food has been swallowed, it does not go straight into the stomach, as in mammals. It is stored for several hours in a sac-like structure in the neck, which is called the crop. For the digestive system to work efficiently, the cockatiel needs a constant, slow trickle of food to enter the stomach. The crop allows the bird to eat a meal and then store the food so that it can pass in small amounts to the stomach.

The crop is visible in baby cockatiels, and the speed with which the crop empties itself is seen as an indicator of good health.

When the food reaches the stomach, it passes through two separate compartments. The first part is a glandular stomach, which is called the proventriculus. This is a thin-walled organ that secretes digestive juices (enzymes) to aid the process of digestion. The second part of the stomach is known as the ventriculus or gizzard. This is a very muscular organ with a hard, rough lining, and it grinds the seed into a paste.

The food passes from the gizzard to the intestines, where the pancreas secretes more digestive enzymes. Once fully broken down, the food is absorbed or stored by the liver. The indigestible wastes are passed through the vent as the dark part of droppings.

It was previously thought that a cockatiel needed a small amount of grit in its diet to allow the gizzard to function properly. However, recent research has found that this is not the case.

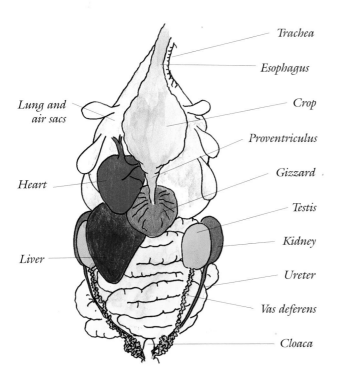

The digestive system

- Trachea
- Esophagus
- Crop
- Proventriculus
- Gizzard
- Testis
- Kidney
- Ureter
- Vas deferens
- Cloaca

Lung and air sacs

Heart

Liver

WILD FOOD

In the wild, a cockatiel's diet is composed of 50 percent grain, 45 percent fresh vegetables, and 5 percent fresh fruit.

Parrots that eat their seed whole, without shelling it, do require grit to aid digestion. Cockatiels that shell the seed before eating it, do not need grit in their diet. In fact, providing grit for cockatiels can lead to digestive problems.

URINARY SYSTEM

Birds excrete urinary wastes in two forms: a liquid urine (the watery part of the droppings), and solid uric acid (the white part of the droppings). The use of solid uric acid is a means of conserving water, and that is why cockatiels, which originate from hot, dry areas, have dry droppings compared to many of the larger, fruit-eating parrots.

PROVIDING SEED

The majority of cockatiels are still fed on a seed-based diet. This comprises a mixture of different seeds. The best mixes to buy are those packaged as parakeet seed or small parakeet mixes. Cockatiels do well on the following seeds:

- Carbohydrate-rich seeds and grains: Canary (Moroccan), millet (white and panic), millet spray (French, Anjou, or Chinese), maize, oats, grouts, wheat, and barley.

Standard seed diets can be fattening and unhealthy for your cockatiel.

- Protein- and fat-rich seeds: Peanut (not salted), pine nut (Russian), linseed, maw, niger, sunflower (striped), safflower, and hemp.

The problems associated with seed-based diets are that they allow the bird to be selective (only eating one type of seed); in time this can lead to nutritional deficiencies (especially vitamin A and calcium), as well as obesity (in high-fat seeds).

High-Fat Diets

Standard seed-based diets fed to caged birds have a fat content of 45 percent, or seven times higher than proprietary chocolate bars. Birds feed to satisfy their energy requirements, so a bird eating a high-fat diet, eats a smaller amount of food and thereby takes in fewer vitamins and minerals.

Many breeders approve of seed-based high-fat diets. The reason for this is that the higher the energy content of the diet, the more the birds are stimulated to breed. While this is advantageous for breeding birds, it is directly contraindicated in pet birds.

OBESITY

Monitor the amount of high-protein and high-fat seeds you feed, as obesity is a common problem among captive birds. Cockatiels love these foods, particularly millet sprays, and will eat them to the exclusion of all other food provided. This means their diet becomes unbalanced, as high-fat foods are deficient in some vitamins and trace elements. The result is an obese cockatiel that becomes lethargic and starts to lose interest in life. If you are concerned that your cockatiel is overweight, cut back on high-protein and high-fat seeds and seek expert advice from your avian veterinarian.

SOAKED SEED

When seed is immersed in water for 24–36 hours, it germinates. The protein content increases, and it is more easily digested. It is only relatively recently that we have started to

Soaked seed has nutritional benefits.

SELL-BY DATES

Make sure the seed you are feeding is fresh and dust-free. The best plan is to buy no more than a month's supply at a time. Beware of moldy seed, and seed that is split and has a sticky sap oozing from it, as this is highly toxic. Seeds should be stored in a place that is cool, dry, and well ventilated.

appreciate the health value of sprouting seeds for our own consumption, but bird keepers have known this for some time.

Once soaked, the seeds must be rinsed thoroughly before they are offered to your cockatiels. They provide a great tonic, and breeders find them especially useful for birds that have youngsters in the nest. However, you must remember to remove all sprouting seeds within a couple of hours. Sprouted seed is a likely carrier of numerous pathenogenic bacteria, and should always be used with caution.

PELLETED DIETS

In recent times, there has been extensive research into feeding pet birds, particularly in the United States. A complete, pelleted diet has been produced, and for many breeders and pet owners it has become a preferred option. It has been discovered that a cockatiel may die as young as five years of age if it is fed a diet that is poorly balanced.

Well-formulated pellet diets are readily available at veterinarians and good-quality pet shops. The advantage of a pellet diet is that no supplements are needed to provide a comprehensive diet for your bird. Wild birds have developed to thrive living outside under the sun. Ultraviolet light in the sun converts vitamin D_3 to activated vitamin D_3, an essential requirement for the calcium metabolism system of birds.

It is important to appreciate that glass or plastics exclude ultraviolet light, so any bird living inside must either be provided with a "full-spectrum lightbulb," which must be changed every six months and placed no more than 3 feet (1 m) above the birds' main perch, or alternatively be provided with activated vitamin D_3 in the diet. Any quality pelleted diet will contain supplementary vitamin D_3.

A quality pelleted diet will contain a range of ingredients, resulting in a balanced diet; the bird in turn is unable to be selective.

Converting a bird to a pelleted diet

The only drawback of the pellet diet is that some cockatiels are not attracted to it and seem to prefer a seed diet, plus fruit and vegetables. In the first instance, you should never attempt to convert a bird to a new diet unless you know that it is fit and healthy, so a checkup first with an experienced bird veterinarian is advisable.

You must commence the process with the following resolution: "I am more stubborn than you are and I am not going to give up," and resolve not to give up for six weeks. If after that time he is still not eating the selected pelleted diet, simply continue but with a different make of food.

Before you start converting to a new food, get the bird used to eating its normal food off a bird mirror laid flat on the bottom of the cage. In this way, every time he goes to make a mouth full of food, he sees another bird doing the same. Eating is a social activity in psittacine birds, so another bird eating encourages your bird to eat.

You must not starve your bird, so allow him to have his normal seed-based diet three times a day for 10 minutes each time. At other times of the day, place your bird's new diet on the mirror (where his normal food would have been), and also provide a selection of fruit or vegetables.

Whenever any member of the family is eating or drinking during the day, you should make a point of eating next to the bird. The bird believes he is a member of your flock, so when he sees you eating he will be encouraged to eat; in this way you are encouraging him to eat his new food.

FRUIT

Cockatiels are not as interested in fruit as some of the larger Parrots from tropical regions, where fruit is a major part of their diet. However, tiels clearly enjoy a variety of different fruit and it has important food value in the form of minerals, vitamin A and vitamin C, which cannot be obtained from seed.

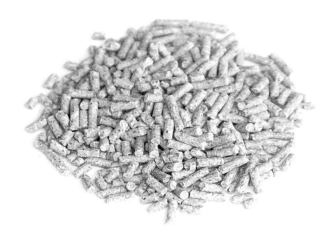

A complete pelleted diet for cockatiels is a popular option with many bird keepers.

Try your cockatiels on different fruit and find out what they like best. The most popular are usually: apple, orange, grape, honeydew melon, kiwi, banana, blackberry, strawberry, elderberry, and peach. Cockatiels also like dried fruit, such as fig and apricot, but these must be soaked first, or they may swell in the bird's digestive system.

Fruit to be avoided include: grapefruit, rhubarb, lemons, and plums.

A BIT AT A TIME

Whenever you are introducing a new item of food to your cockatiels, offer only a little at a time. A sudden glut of a new food will almost inevitably cause digestive problems.

A selection of fruit suitable for cockatiels.

Cockatiels enjoy a variety of vegetables.

VEGETABLES AND GREEN FOOD

Cockatiels generally like a wide selection of vegetables. Favorites include: boiled potatoes, carrots, celery, spinach, beet, corn, broccoli, kale, and asparagus. Make sure all the vegetables are washed thoroughly. Dried vegetables, such as peas and lentils, will be appreciated, but they must be soaked first. Tiels like peppers, both hot and sweet. Unlike us, the parrot's mouth is unaffected by the stinging effect of hot peppers.

Some vegetables should be avoided, as they will cause digestive problems. Do not give your cockatiels cabbage, raw or green potatoes, green beans, or lettuce. Avocado should never be given, as this is highly toxic to birds.

WILD FOODS

Gathering food for your cockatiels adds seasonal variety to their diet, but you must be sure that the food has not been sprayed with pesticides or been exposed to car exhaust fumes if it has grown by the side of the road. Wild food favorites for cockatiels include: dandelion, chickweed, and seeding grasses. Always rinse them well before feeding. Your cockatiel will also appreciate twigs and small branches from fruit trees. These are a source of cellulose fiber and also provide the means of a good play session!

OTHER FOOD

Cockatiels love variety in their diet, and you can introduce some different foods from time to time. Try any of the following: oven-baked bread, small dog biscuits, boiled egg, cheese, yogurt, and plain cakes.

SUPPLEMENTS

To ensure that your cockatiels get all the minerals they need in their diet, it is advisable to provide a mineral block, which contains calcium

Dandelion (far left) and chickweed are two popular wild foods that your cockatiel will appreciate. All wild food should be rinsed well before being offered to cockatiels.

and phosphorous. Calcium can also be obtained from cuttlefish bones. These are truly dual-purpose, as they provide occupation for your cockatiels as well as meeting their nutritional needs.

WATER

Cockatiels come from the arid regions of Australia, and they can withstand hot, dry conditions, but water is still essential. Make sure fresh water is always available. Tap water is fine to use, as long as it is fit for human consumption.

HOW MUCH TO FEED

Cockatiels should have seed available at all times. In order to keep the cage or aviary reasonably clean, it is better to provide a small supply of fresh food twice a day—in the morning and in the evening—first clearing up any leftover food so that it does not rot. Breeding birds will need greater amounts of food, especially if chicks are in the nest (see Chapter 10).

TREATS

There is nothing wrong with giving treats to your cockatiel, especially when training. In fact, it will enhance the bond between you and your birds. But caution must be exercised. It is all too easy to give too many treats or use the wrong type. Choose low-energy treats that are low in fat and high in water content. This includes most fruit and vegetables: broccoli, cauliflower, apple, pear, peach, pineapple, fresh corn, and cottage cheese are all suitable. Foods to avoid include avocado, chocolate, ice cream, potato chips, crackers, pretzels, and high-fat seeds.

WASTE NOT, WANT NOT

Your cockatiel may pick up an item of food, eat a few mouthfuls, and then drop it, letting it fall to the bottom of the cage. In most cases, the cockatiel will ignore dropped items of food and so it will go to waste. To avoid this happening, cut fruit and vegetables into small chunks, and you will find that less will be discarded.

CHAPTER SIX

CARING FOR COCKATIELS

We are lucky that cockatiels are hardy little birds that are easy to care for. However, like all pets, tiels will thrive only if they are kept in clean, hygienic conditions, and if you are aware of their needs. It is essential to provide the following:

- A well-balanced diet that is suitable for cockatiels.
- Exercise and activity to keep your tiel mentally alert and physically fit.
- A suitable environment, which means providing clean, spacious living conditions that have good ventilation and are kept at a constant temperature.
- Routine checks to ensure that your cockatiel is well and not suffering discomfort from overgrown claws or beaks.

DAILY TASKS

The daily care of your cockatiel does not need to take very long, but it should never be

neglected—no matter how busy you are. Always find time to check that your cockatiel appears well (see page 117 for signs of ill health). A healthy bird should be bright, alert, and lively. It should be eating the food you provide, and its droppings should appear normal. You will never regret spending a few minutes observing your cockatiel; if you spot trouble at an early stage, you have a far better chance of solving the problem before it gets serious.

In addition to checking your tiel, you will need to:

- Feed your cockatiel twice a day (see Chapter 5: Healthy Eating).
- Fill the water dish with fresh water, or refill the water bottle.
- Clean the food and water bowls.
- Clear away dead husks from around the seed bowl area.
- Remove fresh food, such as fruit and vegetables, which has not been eaten since the

The bottom of the cage should be cleaned regularly.

last time you fed. If you have hung green food on the side of the cage or aviary, you will need to check that it is still fresh.

- If you have a bath in the cage, you will need to fill it with fresh water.
- Rotate the toys in the cage. Take out some items and replace with one or more different types of toy.
- Remove the lining at the base of the cage and replace with a new lining.
- If you have a playstand, clean the tray beneath it.
- If your cockatiel has spent time outside its cage, check the room and clean up droppings.

WEEKLY TASKS

Once a week you will need to give the cage a thorough cleaning. The best time to do this is when your cockatiel is enjoying time outside its cage.

- Remove the base lining from the cage.
- Remove all fixtures and furnishings from the cage, including food and water bowls, toys, ladders, and perches. You will also need to take out any food you have attached to the cage, such as green food or a cuttlefish bone.
- Prepare a bucket of warm water and add disinfectant. You can buy disinfectant that is safe to use from your avian supply store. Wipe down the cage, using a cloth or a sponge. Pay particular attention to the bars of the cage. Cockatiels have a habit of wiping their beaks on the bars, and this can lead to a buildup of bacteria.
- Prepare a fresh bucket of water and disinfectant, then clean all the fixtures and fittings that go in the cage. Make sure all items are dry before returning them to the cage.
- When the cage is dry, put in a fresh base lining.

HYGIENE ALERT

Keeping your bird clean and free of dust will be good for it, but it will also reduce the chance of any family member developing *allergic alveolitis*, a condition in which humans become allergic to the protein from bird feathers.

Also remember to always wash your hands before and after attending to your cleaning chores. The same applies when you are feeding or handling your cockatiels.

- If you have a playstand, give it a thorough washing at the same time.
- Check your supplies of seed or pellet food to ensure that the food is fresh and has not gone past its sell-by date.
- Check toys for signs of wear and tear.

LOOKING GOOD

You will know if your cockatiel is feeling well, if it is looking good. A healthy cockatiel has a nicely rounded body, and its feathers are sleek and held close to the body. Feathers come in several different types:

Contour feathers

These cover the surface of the cockatiel, giving the bird its general shape and color. They are subdivided into flight (tail and wing) and body feathers.

- Body feathers are round to oval in shape, and have a small, soft quill.
- The wing flight feathers, known as remiges, are elongated with a strong, thick quill. Remiges are divided into primary and secondary feathers.
  1. *Primary feathers:* These are attached to the metacarpal bone (below the wrist) on each wing. They are responsible for forward movement in flight.
  2. *Secondary feathers:* These are attached from the wrist inward, toward the body, ending in the elbow. These feathers provide lift in flight.
- The tail flight feathers are known as retrices.
- The base of both remiges and retrices are

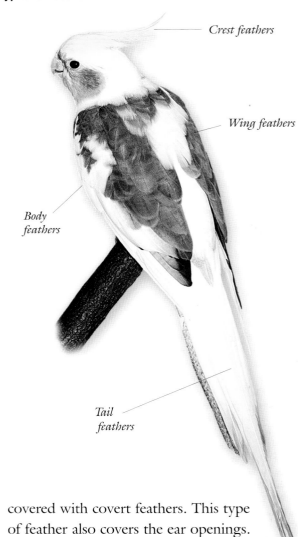

Types of feather

Crest feathers

Wing feathers

Body feathers

Tail feathers

covered with covert feathers. This type of feather also covers the ear openings.
- The glamorous head feathers, known as crest feathers, are used for display.

Down feathers

These feathers provide insulation against the cold. A cockatiel has a thin skin and lacks the fatty layer that is found in most mammals. As a result, a cockatiel would lose body heat rapidly if it were not for the small, fluffy down feathers. Unlike the contour feathers, the down feathers are not waterproof and play no part in flight.

Powder-down feathers are specialized down feathers, which disintegrate to produce a powder that is spread throughout the plumage as a dry lubricant. The lubricant acts as an aid to preening as well as being a waterproof agent. Cockatiels, along with African Greys, Cockatoos, and Macaws, have more powder-down feathers than most other members of the psittacine family, which is why their beaks tend to be gray and powdery rather than shiny.

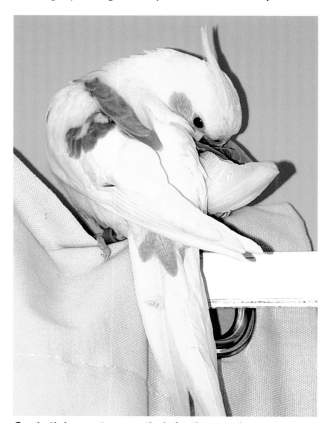

Cockatiels must preen their feathers to keep them clean and healthy.

PREENING

Cockatiels need to keep their feathers in good shape; they do this by preening. The cockatiel has a preen gland, which is a small moundlike area over the rump. It has an opening that is surrounded by a tuft of fine feathers. The gland releases an oily wax that the cockatiel uses to condition its feathers. You will see a tiel turning its head to its rump and then running its beak through its feathers. The oily wax helps to make the feathers insulting and waterproof. It is also thought that the secretion of the preen gland may have antibacterial qualities, as simple skin infections are very rare in birds.

BATHING

All birds benefit from bathing; it helps to keep feathers clean and it also encourages preening. Clean plumage has another advantage, too. It makes it easier for a bird to maneuver its feathers so they can be used to regulate body temperature. When a cockatiel is kept at a constant temperature, it will hold its feathers close to its body. However, if the temperature drops, the cockatiel will fluff up its feathers to keep an insulating cavity of warm air against the skin.

Pet birds that are kept in a home environment are subjected to a very dry atmosphere, and feathers may become brittle and dry. If you provide a bath (see page 34), your cockatiel will enjoy splashing around in the water. Some cockatiels prefer being sprayed. You can do this using the type of spray that is used for watering plants. The best time to spray is when your cockatiel is perched outside its cage. Both the bath water and spray water should be lukewarm.

Ideally, you should bathe or spray your tiel two or three times a week.

Cockatiels need to be provided with a bath, or they should be sprayed regularly.

MOLTING

The feathers of adult birds are replaced at regular intervals throughout their lives. This process is known as molting. In the wild, molting is stimulated by changes in day length, and this usually occurs in the spring, in the fall, and after breeding. Pet birds that are kept in a home environment are not exposed to this natural stimulation and they tend to have a continuous, partial molt, rather than replacing all their feathers at the same time.

When a cockatiel molts, a new feather emerges from a small mound in the base of the feather follicle, which is known as the dermal papilla. The new feather grows downward, pushing out the old feather. In the early stages, the new feather is soft, fragile, and filled with blood; fully grown feathers on either side of the new feather serve to protect it. Once the feather is fully developed, the blood vessels retract, leaving a tough, mature feather. Growing new feathers puts great strain on a bird. Many bird keepers will provide additional nutrition if their cockatiels are going through a complete molt.

WING CLIPPING

This involves trimming the primary flight feathers on the wings to curtail a cockatiel's flight. The object of the exercise is not to stop the cockatiel from flying, but to prevent it from gaining height at speed. Most pet owners would agree that there is nothing better than seeing a cockatiel fly—but there is nothing worse than losing a cockatiel as a result of an escape accident, or because of an accident when the bird injures itself, or ingests something that is poisonous.

Many bird keepers believe that wing clipping is the only safe option if you are keeping captive birds, for the following reasons:

• A clipped bird will never escape from its home.
• Accidents, such as crashing into windows, are avoided.
• It is far easier to hand-train a bird with clipped wings.
• Clipping wings is not a painful process.
• The bird is not frustrated, as it still has limited flight.

There are some bird keepers who are against wing clipping, believing that it is a bird's natural

WING CLIPPING

Clip the long primary flight feather. If you clip the first four feathers, the bird retains the ability for limited flight.

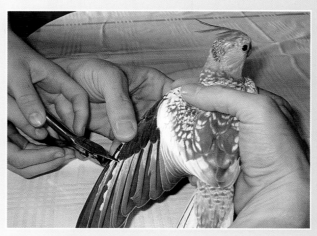

Clip one feather at a time.

The first feather has been clipped.

Check the quill of each feather before clipping. Mature feathers should have a white quill. New or young feathers may still have a blue quill (containing blood) and should not be cut.

The wing after clipping.

right to fly, and accidents can be avoided if a room is properly bird-proofed. If you want to discuss the subject of wing clipping in more detail, contact an avian veterinarian, who will be able to outline the pros and cons.

The procedure

In most cases, the primary flight feathers on both wings are trimmed. Some aviculturists will not clip the two outer feathers, as they mask the clipped feathers when the wings are folded. The secondary flight feathers are never clipped. The feathers will be replaced when the bird next molts, so wing clipping must be carried out on a regular basis if you want to continue restricting your cockatiel's flying ability.

In the past, birds were clipped on one wing only. This is now considered unacceptable, as the bird is never able to land in the direction it heads for; it can fly only in an arc. Eventually, the bird loses confidence and gives up flying altogether, which is an entirely unnatural state of affairs.

Some breeders routinely clip the wings of young chicks before they are sold. Ideally, the young bird will be given the opportunity to fly and develop its flight muscles in the safety of the breeder's home.

Call in the experts

When your cockatiel's wings need clipping, you should ask an avian veterinarian or an experienced bird keeper to do the job for you. The wings should be clipped gently and evenly. Ideally, they should be clipped in gradual stages so that the bird can adjust to the resulting flight restrictions. Over-zealous or uneven clipping is very stressful for a bird, and, in severe cases, it has led to self-mutilation (see page 99). It is also important to bear in mind that if a bird is unbalanced in flight, it could fall to the ground, resulting in serious injury.

TRIMMING NAILS

In the wild, a cockatiel naturally wears down its nails by perching on different branches, as well as being on different surfaces when feeding at ground level. The caged cockatiel has no such opportunities. As we have seen, it is helpful to provide a variety of perches, which will ensure that your cockatiel's feet do not become sore or calloused. But this will not be sufficient to keep the nails in trim.

Trimming nails is not difficult, but you will need to be shown the correct procedure. The best plan is to seek the assistance of an experienced bird keeper or to book an appointment with your avian veterinarian. When you have watched the procedure a couple of times, you will probably feel confident to tackle the job, but you will always need to enlist a helper to hold the cockatiel while you trim its nails.

Step by step

Prepare your cockatiel for nail trimming by handling it regularly. When the bird is on a perch, you can touch its feet and maybe lift one foot at a time. You can use the opportunity to check the underside of the feet, making sure there is no sign

 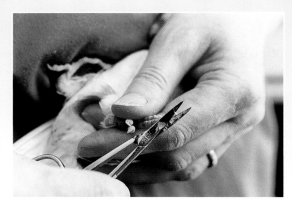

If the nails do not wear down naturally, they will need to be trimmed.

of soreness. When you are ready to start nail trimming, adopt the following procedure:

- Gently wrap the cockatiel in a towel. Talk to the bird to reassure it.
- One person should hold the bird, confined in the towel, while the other trims the nails.
- You can use a sharp pair of nail scissors, or you can use the guillotine type of nail clippers. The type used for small dogs and cats is suitable for cockatiels.
- Trim the tip of each nail. It is far better to be cautious and trim a little at a time. If you trim too much, you risk cutting the blood vessel that runs partway down the nail. This will result in bleeding, and will be sore and uncomfortable for your cockatiel.
- If necessary, the bleeding can be stopped by applying styptic powder, corn flour, or soap.
- When nails are trimmed regularly, the blood vessel shrinks back, making the job easier.

Most tiels learn to accept nail trimming without too much fuss when they find it does not hurt. If you do not feel confident about trimming your cockatiel's nails, continue to seek the help of an expert. If a cockatiel associates nail trimming with discomfort because you have caused a nail to bleed, you will end up with a battle every time the bird's nails need cutting.

Do not neglect this task. If a cockatiel's nails grow too long, it may find it difficult to perch, or a nail may get caught while the cockatiel is climbing up the bars of its cage, resulting in a painful injury.

BEAK TRIMMING

If your cockatiel is young and healthy, and has plenty of chewing material, the beak should wear down naturally. Problems may occur if the upper and lower portions of the beak do not line up correctly. In this case, part of the beak does not wear down and continues to grow. In the worst cases, this makes eating impossible.

Misalignment may be an inherited fault, which is why you should pay close attention to the beak when you are buying a cockatiel.

But it can also be caused by a bored bird that continually bites on the bars of its cage.

If your cockatiel has difficulty eating, and you suspect the beak is causing problems, book an appointment with your veterinarian, who will be able to reshape the beak. Do not attempt this task yourself. If you cut into the corium, the living core of the beak, profuse bleeding will result.

REHOMING

When you buy a cockatiel, you are obviously planning to look after it and care for it for the duration of its life. However, situations can change, and you may find that you can no longer provide your cockatiel with a suitable home. This may be because of a job move, a change in your family situation, or as a result of ill health.

Moving homes can be very distressing for a tiel that is happily settled, particularly if it is an older bird. As a responsible bird keeper, your job is to ensure a safe future for your cockatiel.

You may know someone who is prepared to take in your bird, but be wary of this option. A friend may be well meaning, but they may not understand what is involved in looking after a cockatiel. In this case, your cockatiel may be at risk from poor care, or it may be passed onto another home, which may be even worse.

You can try posting a notice at your veterinarian's office, where you will have a better chance of finding a knowledgeable owner, or you can make contact with local cockatiel societies and find out if anyone is prepared to take on another bird.

There are also a number of Parrot rescue sanctuaries, as well as those specifically for cockatiels, which may be prepared to take on your cockatiel. For more information on cockatiel rescue, log onto *www.cockatiel rescue.org*, which has links with organizations in the United States and worldwide.

BEST FRIENDS

Owning several pet birds and running a Parrot rescue group means that Athena Jeske from Erie, Colorado, knows all about the bond that can exist between people and their feathered friends. But one of the most special relationships she has seen began the day she took in two cockatiels.

"Before they came to us, Moe and Curley were kept in their cage full-time and were never given any human interaction beyond cage cleaning and feeding. Moe was plucking Curley's head, so we had to separate them. My son, Cedric, agreed to have Moe in his room, even though Moe was mean, bit all the time, and acted as if he hated people.

"Cedric was fascinated by Moe from the moment we brought the little bird home. Cedric was used to tame cockatiels, and

Continued on page 68

BEST FRIENDS

Continued from page 67
meeting one that was a biter was a new exper-ience. He knew that cockatiels could be tame, he knew that they could talk, and he knew that they could enjoy hanging out with people. So, Cedric took over Moe's daily care, helping the bird to understand that people can be kind and fun. He would sit and quietly read to him so that Moe got used to his voice. Cedric would move with exaggerated slowness in order not to frighten him. He always called out ahead of him before he walked by Moe's cage, so he didn't startle him.

"Eventually, Cedric asked if he could allow Moe's wings to grow in fully, to allow him flight. Cedric felt that part of Moe's problem was that he was easily frightened, and if he could fly away from things that spooked him, he might feel safer. Because he had shown such dedication to providing a safe and healthy environment for the bird, we agreed to try this—and Cedric's instinct proved to be true. Once Moe could fly away from everyone, he stopped attacking and biting people. Moe grew friendly with us in a standoffish way. He'd whistle with us or accept treats, but he never was comfortable with us as he was with Cedric. That little bird acted like the sun rose and set on Cedric.

"As time went by and the bond between Cedric and Moe deepened, Cedric introduced some trick training. He taught Moe how to hang off a stick, how to climb into his shirt when he was frightened, and he also taught him recall, which is coming when called. Moe wanted to be with Cedric so badly that he was always flying to him, so Cedric trained it to be a behavior. He also taught Moe how to speak. He would say 'Moe' and, 'Cedric' and 'Good Bird!'. Moe taught Cedric a few things, too! Cedric didn't know how to whistle when he got Moe, and because Moe enjoyed whistling so much, Cedric practiced and practiced until he could do it, just so he could whistle with his bird.

"One incident that really shows the bond between Cedric and Moe happened one night when Cedric was staying the night at a friend's house. My husband, Michael, walked into Cedric's room one night to feed Moe, who was out of his cage. He was a very talented escape artist and we were always having to find new ways to lock his cage to prevent escapes. My husband quickly closed the bedroom door and tried using the whistle that Cedric had taught Moe to come to, so that he could get him and put him back in his cage. Moe refused. My husband called me and tried sneaking up on Moe. Moe flew to the top of his play station, where it hung from the ceiling. For 10 minutes we tried getting Moe to come to us, and he just flew from one spot in the room to another. Eventually, I drove to Cedric's friend's house and explained that I needed to borrow my son for a few minutes. As soon as Cedric walked in the bedroom Moe flew to his shoulder and said 'Cedric... ahhhhh' in such a tired voice, we all had to laugh.

"One of the saddest days for us all was the day Moe passed away. Cedric came home from school and found Moe lying in the bottom of his cage. He came to me and said 'I think there is something wrong with Moe.' He had huge tears in his eyes, and I knew right then that Moe had gone. He was an old bird when we took him in, and he had already lived longer than the veterinarian thought he would. I went in and picked him up, and confirmed that he had passed away. We cried together, and I pulled a tail feather from Moe that Cedric could keep. Then we went outside together, buried Moe, sat together, and said a prayer. Cedric went back inside to spend some quiet time thinking about his friend. He was very quiet and subdued for a few days, and he refused to allow me to remove Moe's cage from his room. It took him about a week to be ready for that, and then he took it himself to wash and put away. I think he just needed time to be able to accept that Moe was not coming back.

"Despite the pain that Cedric experienced on Moe's death, the benefits he has gained from caring for Moe have been enormous. Cedric learned how to care for another living creature— to clean up after it, feed and water it, and give it attention. Cedric learned that loving something can be frustrating, because even if you love it with all your heart, it is still going to be what it is, and only time and patience can help change bad habits. His love for Moe was so deep that he wanted everything to be the very best for him, and he worked hard to provide for him. Cedric built Moe toys, bought him treats, and made sure that he got a minimum of two hours of attention a day each and every day, even if that meant cutting short playtime with his friends. Cedric's bond with Moe is something most people never get to experience in their lifetime. He is a naturally exuberant young man, who moves quickly and talks loudly. Something about that bird brought out the gentle, soft, sweet side of him. He managed to take a bird who was already old and untamed and helped him become a loving, happy creature.

"Following Moe's death, Cedric was devastated for a while, and he was unable to interact with any animal. He needed time to understand that kind of pain and he is a better person for that lesson. He is very giving and caring, and he takes time every day to show his love to the people and animals that matter so much to him."

Best buddy: Moe with all his toys.

CHAPTER SEVEN

UNDERSTANDING COCKATIELS

If you are new to bird keeping, you will find it helpful to understand a little about how your cockatiel's body works and how your pet sees the world. This will enable you to provide for your tiel's needs and you will also have some valuable clues as to how your bird is feeling.

HEARING

Birds do not have external ears. They have small holes, located on either side of the head, behind and below the level of the outer corner of the eyes, which serve as an opening to the ear canal. You cannot see the holes, as they are covered by feathers. The ear canal leads to the eardrum and the middle ear, which is similar to the hearing system of mammals.

Cockatiels have an acute sense of hearing, as, in the wild, they have to communicate with each other over long distances. They also have the ability to distinguish between small differences in frequency. As a result, tiels are very sensitive to sound and have a particular dislike of loud noises.

SIGHT

Sight is the most important of the senses for birds, as their survival in the wild depends on spotting predators and finding food. Compared to us, parrots, including cockatiels, have large eyes, which are similar in structure to our own. Their eyes are situated on the sides of their head, giving them panoramic vision. Cockatiels fly at speed, and they have developed the ability to process visual images very quickly. A cockatiel can absorb more than 1,200 images per second, compared to a human, who can deal with just 16 over the same time span.

Tiels have good color vision, and it is believed that they can see far into both the ultraviolet spectrum and the infrared, which means that they can see colors that we cannot see. However, they have poor night vision, and this may cause problems with night frights (see page 102).

Cockatiels have large eyes in relation to their size.

SMELL
Like most birds, the cockatiel has a poorly developed sense of smell. However, they are highly sensitive to smoke in the atmosphere.

TASTE
In common with other parrots, the cockatiel has a much lower number of taste buds than mammals. They are situated on the roof of the mouth, the floor of the mouth, in the throat, and there are a few on the tongue.

Although taste buds are relatively few in number, taste still seems to play a part in a cockatiel's everyday life. Tiels have favorite foods, and they certainly have dislikes, as has been witnessed by anyone who has had to give medication to their cockatiel.

TOUCH
The cockatiel uses its beak for investigating new objects, as well as to manipulate seeds within its mouth so they are in the perfect position for cracking and dehusking. The cockatiel also uses its feet to pick up objects and manipulate them.

COCKATIEL BEHAVIOR
With some pets, such as cats and dogs, it is very easy to read their body language and understand how they are feeling. You are unlikely to be confused by a dog's wagging tail or a cat's contented purr. With birds, it can be a little more complicated, and you will need to observe your cockatiels closely in order to get on their wavelength. Once you know what to look for, and what certain sounds mean, you will be well on the way to having a full understanding of tiel behavior.

Routine activities
There are a number of routine behaviors that a cockatiel will perform on a regular basis. They are all instinctive and show that your tiel is contented and functioning normally.

Preening
It is figured that most cockatiels devote at least two hours a day to preening. A cockatiel runs each feather through its beak, from the base to the tip, to straighten it and to remove dust and dirt. It will keep turning its head to its rear to get oil from its preen gland. In order to get oil on its head feathers, the cockatiel rubs its head directly over the gland.

Preening is also a social activity. Tiels that are caged together often present themselves to each other for preening. If your cockatiel trusts you, it may offer to "preen" your hair.

Regurgitating

Cockatiels that have formed a close bond often feed each other by regurgitating small amounts of partly digested food. A bird will bob its head up and down in order to bring up food from the crop and then deposit it directly into the other bird's mouth. This is how parents feed their chicks in the wild and it is recognized as a sign of affection between paired birds.

In some cases, a tiel will regurgitate over a favorite toy, or even in close proximity to a favorite person whom it regards as a "mate."

Sleeping

A cockatiel needs 10 to 12 hours of sleep each night to stay healthy. When a cockatiel is sleeping, it will generally pull up one leg and twist its head to bury its beak in its back feathers. A tiel that is deprived of sleep may show signs of irritation and bad temper, and if this continues, the bird may become ill.

If you are keeping your cockatiel in a room that is used in the evening, it may suffer from being exposed to too much light and activity. The solution is to fit a dimmer light where the cage is located or to place a thin cover over the cage, so your cockatiel will be able to rest.

When a cockatiel is sleeping, it should not be disturbed.

Beak wiping

After eating, and on other occasions, a cockatiel rubs its beak on a perch or on the bars of the cage. This is a way of cleaning the beak and keeping it in good order. A cockatiel may also use this behavior to tell another bird that it has intruded on its personal territory.

Feather shaking

A cockatiel gives its feathers a vigorous shake several times a day. This often follows preening, when the bird is getting rid of dust and making sure its feathers are in place. It also seems to be a way of easing tension or ending a period of intense concentration.

Stretching

Just like us, a cockatiel feels the need to stretch in order to ease tension and stiffness, particularly if it has been perched in the same position for some time. The bird extends one leg backward, and, at the same time, it extends the wing on the same side backward. A cockatiel may also lift both wings to stretch them.

A cockatiel will stretch when it has been perched in one position for a while. It may also spread its wings when it is being sprayed.

Yawning

This may be a sign of fatigue but it also may indicate that the air in the atmosphere is stale and the cockatiel is suffering from lack of oxygen. If you see your cockatiel yawn repeatedly, you should air the room.

Sneezing

A cockatiel sneezes to clear its nasal passages in exactly the same way as we do. Sneezing is a cause for concern only if it is accompanied by nasal discharge. If this is the case, you should seek advice from an avian veterinarian.

Whistling, singing

Communicating by sound is very important to cockatiels. They are most likely to be vocal at dawn and at dusk, but a happy cockatiel will always be ready to burst into song or to mimic sounds. A cockatiel that has learned to talk will repeat words or phrases for its own entertainment!

Chattering

Chattering or crowing is usually heard at dusk when cockatiels are settling down for the night. It is thought to be a way of making their presence known to other birds, as well as to cement relationships among the flock. A contented tiel may chatter at other times during the day. This is usually muted, but if you listen carefully, you may hear your cockatiel practicing its talking skills.

Reading the signs

In addition to routine activities, cockatiels also react to specific situations, and, with practice, you will be able to interpret your tiel's moods. This is not simply a matter of interest. If your cockatiel is distressed or unhappy, it will fail to thrive. Cockatiels are sensitive birds and will quickly become depressed if they are kept in unsuitable or stressful conditions.

Tongue clicking

A rapid clicking of the tongue against the beak is a friendly signal, inviting closer contact. Cockatiels use this behavior toward other birds and also when interacting with people. The cockatiel is basically saying, "I want to be your friend; I pose no threat to you."

Beak clicking

A sharp, consistent click means a cockatiel feels threatened. The bird is generally trying to defend its territory or a particular object. A cockatiel may also stretch its neck and raise a foot in an attempt to intimidate the "intruder." If a cockatiel is showing this type of behavior, keep away, or you may get bitten (see page 97).

Beak grinding

A cockatiel scrapes its lower beak against its upper beak when it is feeling safe and secure. It is most often heard when a bird is relaxed and is about to sleep. Some cockatiels grind their beaks while they are asleep.

Purring

A low-volume purr is a sign of contentment. A purring cockatiel appears relaxed and its feathers may be fluffed up.

Growling

A sure sign of aggression, growling is sometimes accompanied by dilated pupils and raised feathers at the back of the neck. Do not approach a cockatiel that is showing this type of behavior.

Barking

Your cockatiel is not necessarily mimicking a dog. Cockatiels may "bark" with excitement when they are chattering. A bird may also bark to express dominance over its cagemate.

With experience, you can read cockatiel behavior. This cockatiel is angry and may well bite.

Screaming

This is not a typical sound for a cockatiel. An occasional screech of excitement—or complaint—is not a cause for concern. But if a tiel screeches continuously, it is a sign of distress. It is most likely to be heard if a cockatiel is caged alone for long periods and has no occupation (see page 98).

Craning the neck

If a cockatiel is interested in something, it will crane its neck to get a better look. It will generally hold its body very still and you may see a widening of the eyes.

Lowering the head

If a cockatiel is standing still with its head lowered and its feathers puffed out, it is asking for a scratch. Make sure the body posture is relaxed, as the crouch stance (see page 76) is a sign of aggression. If you read the signs, it is not difficult to interpret the cockatiel's intentions.

If a cockatiel lowers its head below perch level and quivers its wings, it is about to take flight. This stance may also be adopted by a tiel seeking attention.

Shaking the head

This is usually seen as a "snaking" movement as the cockatiel moves its head from side to side. The tiel is expressing excitement or asking for attention. It may also be used in display behavior (see page 78).

Head bobbing

This may be seen when a cockatiel is hungry and asking to be fed. It is often seen in hand-reared chicks.

Drooping wings

This is often seen in young cockatiels that are not adept at tucking in their wings. If a cockatiel has had a bath or a spray, it may hold its wings in a drooping position to dry them (see page 62).

An overheated tiel may hold its wings outward in an attempt to cool down. If you see a cockatiel sitting on the bottom of the cage with drooping wings, it is almost certainly sick and you should seek veterinary advice.

Flipping wings

A cockatiel may flip one or both wings as a sign of irritation. It will also do this to realign its feathers prior to preening.

Drumming wings

This is a way of exercising and stretching the wings and will often be seen when a cockatiel is released from its cage. The cockatiel takes up a position and may drum its wings so strongly that it lifts itself a few inches.

Quivering wings

This is a sign of nervousness or distrust, and you may see it in the early stages of hand-training. Take time to reassure your cockatiel before you attempt to make contact. If the whole body is quivering, the cockatiel is probably trying to adjust to a marked change of temperature in the environment. If you have a breeding pair of cockatiel, you may see a tiel quiver its wings in order to "solicit" a response from its partner.

Tail fanning

This is a sign of aggression. A cockatiel fans its tail when it is angry or if it is showing displeasure at a particular activity.

Tail wagging

A quick wag of the tail feathers, back and forth, is a sign of contentment. A cockatiel may wag its tail when it is enjoying a favorite activity.

Crouching

An aggressive cockatiel lowers its head and points it forward. The tail feathers are fanned and the body feathers are raised. Flashing eyes often accompany this posture; it is very clear that the bird is angry, as opposed to the relaxed

THE CREST

The cockatiel's crest is one of its most glamorous features, but it serves an important purpose in tiel communication. The position of the crest tells you how a bird is feeling. A young cockatiel will hold its crest erect most of the time. It is only when the bird starts to mature that it uses its crest to signal moods.

A crest that is held erect.
The cockatiel is alert and ready for action.

A crest that lies flat, with only the tips of the feathers pointing upward.
The cockatiel is relaxed and contented.

The crest is pointing straight up, with the tips of the feathers slightly forward.
The cockatiel is startled or agitated.

The crest plays an important part in tiel communication.

The crest is held straight back.
The cockatiel is angry, and will usually hold its beak open and hiss at the same time.

stance and lowered head of a cockatiel inviting a scratch (see page 75).

Panting

This is never a good sign in cockatiels. It usually means the bird is overheated or has over-exerted itself. If you see a bird panting, check that its cage is not in direct sunlight and make sure that fresh drinking water is available. If the bird continues to pant, seek veterinary advice.

Dilating pupils

This can be a hard behavioral sign to read, as it can indicate a variety of states including excitement, nervousness, pleasure, or aggression. The key is to look at the other behaviors that accompany the "flashing eyes."

If a cockatiel is aggressive, it will have dilated pupils but it will also fan its tail, stand tall, and look threatening, telling you—or another bird—to keep away.

Cockatiels are territorial, and if a bird feels threatened, it will express its feelings verbally and with body language.

Display behavior

When cockatiels are trying to get a mate, or even when a same-sex pair is forming a bond, they will display to each other. This is a form of attraction and it is also used to cement a pair bond.

Display behavior includes ruffling the head feathers and fanning the tail. The wings may be fully extended, and the cock will often circle the hen with tiny, strutting steps, raising his crest. A bonded pair of cockatiels will eat, sleep, and perch together. They will preen each other and will also regurgitate food for each other.

FEATHERED FAMILY

Cockatiels make fascinating pets, and owners can learn a lot about their birds by observing their behavior. This can be particularly absorbing if you own several birds, as Carol from Omaha, Nebraska, keeper of three cockatiels and a flock of parakeets, has witnessed.

"I have always loved birds," says Carol. "I started with some parakeets, which I found very soothing to watch. But the first time I held a cockatiel, and felt how gentle it was, I fell in love with them.

"At the moment I have three cockatiels: Truus, a 21-month-old female; Lovey, a 15-month-old female; and Vader, a 13-month-old male. I fell in love with Truus when I went to a breeder to look at her cockatiels. There was a large cage of 'older' birds against one wall. As we walked past, one bird started calling and climbing across the cage. She kept calling and calling and finally I asked about her. She was nine months old and had been considered for breeding because of her sweet, gentle nature, but her breeder had decided against it. I got to hold this little bird and we immediately bonded. When I put her back in the cage she seemed heartbroken. She kept calling and calling as we walked away. The next day I went back and bought her, along with Lovey, whom my eight-year-old daughter had fallen in love with.

"Each of my birds has its own unique qualities. Truus is very much a 'people bird.' She really doesn't care for the company of other birds. She wants to be with people all the time, so that she can get skritches (a soothing scratch on the back of the neck), attention, and affection. She loves to play with people, and her favorite game is 'Uh Oh,' where she drops things from whatever she's sitting on so that you have to lean over to get it for her. She gets very jealous of attention given to the other birds. When I first got her she would even get jealous of attention given to other people. But once she learned that they gave good skritches and had treats to offer, she overcame that problem.

"Lovey is more of a 'bird's bird.' She's very reserved and doesn't care to be touched. Nor does she like to hang out with people. She prefers to play with toys and to eat and socialize with Vader, her mate.

"Vader is the real character of the cockatiel flock. He was three months old when I got him. A standard gray cockatiel, his bearing reminded me of Darth Vader—hence his name. I started teaching him songs by whistling to him and he mastered "The Imperial March" within a few weeks, as well as the Darth Vader breathing. He wolf whistles, whistles several other tunes we've taught him, and he even started talking on his own. He's also picked up sounds from the other birds, has learned to call the dog, and makes up beautiful little songs of his own.

"Vader likes people but he doesn't enjoy being touched or skritched with the hands. Nose skritches and kisses are fine. He loves to sit on your shoulders, where he's right in the action.

Continued on page 80

A bird's bird: Lovey is wary of people.

FEATHERED FAMILY

Continued from page 79

If someone whistles or sings, he's right there, listening to them, and will run off the other tiels so that he can have the person's undivided attention. He loves kisses and will kiss me when he wants me to sing.

"Although the three tiels have distinct personalities, they all get along together very well. The funniest thing to see is when they want skritches from each other. They'll bow their heads and each will get lower and lower until finally one will give in and skritch the head of the other for a brief moment, then expect the other to do the same. They sometimes get really frustrated with each other and fight. Usually fights are over the 'skritch me' game.

"Vader and Lovey are pair-bonded, and Vader is very defensive of Lovey. The cockatiels share their flight cages with the parakeets, and if any of the parakeets get too close to Lovey, Vader will run them off, wings spread and beak wide open. I remember when Vader first started taking an interest in Lovey. He was about nine months old and just starting to realize that Lovey was a hen and he liked her a lot. Sitting on the same straw wreath, he would lean closer to her and sing, with his wings all heart-shaped. She would move slightly away, all coy and shy. The more she inched away, the closer he leaned toward her and spread his wings out. This continued until the wreath rolled, resulting in Lovey being flung off and Vader losing his balance. Oh, my word, it was funny! I'm delighted I managed to record it on video.

"Tiels are very gentle birds and my daughter adores them. They make fantastic and absorbing companions. I'd definitely recommend them as pets, but only if the prospective owner is prepared to learn about their behavior beforehand. It's also important to keep learning once you've got them and are interacting with them. The more you know why they do what they do, the more you can communicate with them and they with you, and the more enjoyment you'll both have."

CHAPTER EIGHT

TRAINING COCKATIELS

The cockatiel is one of the smaller members of the Parrot family, so you may consider that training is relatively unimportant. It is true that a small, untrained cockatiel is unlikely to be as difficult to handle as a large, untrained macaw. But a tiel that has not learned to live with people will give little pleasure and can be a real noise nuisance.

STARTING RIGHT

In most cases, a cockatiel will be around eight weeks old when it first arrives home. It is important to bear in mind that you are dealing with a young bird that has only recently gained its independence. Even the most outgoing cockatiel is bound to feel vulnerable at this time, and you need to give the bird a sense of security.

Cockatiels are flock birds and respond to the concept of leadership. Right from the start, you need to see yourself in the role of flock leader, making the decisions for your cockatiel. Obviously, you will be a kind and caring leader,

and all the decisions you make will be in the best interests of your pet bird, but do not be afraid to make house rules and keep to them. Like small children, cockatiels need to know their boundaries, and they will be much happier if they understand what is acceptable behavior.

A young, just-weaned tiel can be demanding and will use its voice to get your attention. This may be endearing initially, but in no time you will be literally at your cockatiel's beck and call. Although you want to reassure your cockatiel, you do not need to baby it too much. From the start, make sure your tiel has time alone. There may be protests to begin with, but if this does not produce results, then the cockatiel will learn to settle. A cockatiel must have the confidence to spend time alone; otherwise it will become stressed every time you leave the room. This is more likely to happen to a lone cockatiel. But separation anxiety can develop very quickly—even in the short period when you are settling in one cockatiel before buying a companion bird.

FREE-FLYING

Once your cockatiel has had a chance to settle in its new home, you will want to give it the opportunity to exercise outside its cage. Even if your tiel has had its wings clipped, this is a scenario that must be managed with great care. A young bird is curious and wants to investigate everything it sees. If the cockatiel can fly—even if its flight is limited—it will need to get used to maneuvring in a confined space.

Before you allow your cockatiel to fly outside the cage, you need to check that the room is safe and secure. Hopefully, you will have prepared the room for free-flying before your bird's arrival (see page 36).

To begin with, your cockatiel may fly no further than to the top of its cage. In fact, many tiels enjoy spending time on the cage top; it gives them a good vantage point and they feel safe and secure at their home base. If you have a playstand, your cockatiel will adopt this as a home away from home and will head straight for its second base when released from the cage. As your cockatiel grows in confidence, it will explore the room and discover good places to perch. For the first few flying sessions, stay with your cockatiel so you can be confident that the bird does not get into mischief.

Quality time

When your cockatiel is used to being free, there is no reason why it should not spend extended periods outside the cage. As a minimum requirement, a tiel should have at least one hour outside its cage per day, but the longer a bird can

Extreme caution must be exercised if your cockatiel is allowed out of the cage and given the opportunity to fly.

spend enjoying its freedom, the happier it will be. If you have a playstand, and some perches arranged around the room, you will be able to keep track of your cockatiel's movements.

Cockatiels often feed on the ground when they are in the wild, and, as a result, they are quite happy to wander around at floor level. Bear this in mind when your cockatiel is outside the cage, in order to avoid stepping on it and causing injury.

Foraging enrichment

This is an excellent way of providing your tiel with mental stimulation when it is outside the cage.

• First, find out what the bird's favorite food item is, then remove it from its normal diet.
• Create eight to ten hiding places around the house, where on a given day food might be hidden. Food is, however, hidden in only two or three sites each day.

With practice, a cockatiel will learn to return to you.

• Next, teach the bird where these hiding holes are. Then each day the owner will at some point let the bird out of its cage, encouraging it to hunt around the house for the hidden food.

This activity stimulates a bird's natural foraging activity and will occupy it happily for at least an hour each day.

RETURNING TO THE CAGE

When it is time to return your cockatiel to the cage, adopt the following procedure.

• Approach the tiel quietly and offer a treat. Hold the back of your hand, or an outstretched index finger, slightly above your cockatiel's feet.
• The tiel should be attracted by the treat and step onto your hand or finger. Walk back to the cage and place your hand in the cage so the cockatiel can fly back inside.

• You may need to be patient until your tiel accepts what you are doing. The secret is to choose a really tasty treat, so the cockatiel has a good reason for giving up its freedom and coming to you.
• If the cockatiel keeps flying away when you are taking it back to the cage, try dimming the lights in the room. In most cases, the cockatiel will stay on your hand until it is returned to the cage.
• As a last resort, you can cup your hands over the bird, and carry it back to the cage. But most tiels will learn to return "home" without major protests.

CALLING YOUR COCKATIEL

With training, a cockatiel will respond to its name being called, particularly if you have chosen a simple name composing of one or two syllables. Many bird keepers call their cockatiels or use a special whistle, which means "come to me" or "home time."

If you want to train your tiel to respond to its name or to a whistle, make sure you have a tasty treat ready.

• Call your cockatiel's name or use a whistle. The moment the cockatiel looks in your direction, reward it with a treat.
• Repeat this exercise, rewarding the tiel every time it looks at you when you whistle or call its name. In this way, the cockatiel will learn to associate its name or the whistle with something it likes, such as the treat.

DIZZY HEIGHTS

What do you do if your cockatiel has perched high on the curtain rod and is out of reach? Fortunately, you do not have to go mountaineering in order to get to your bird. All you need is a long pole, such as a piece of dowelling, about 3 feet (1 m) in length. You can then position the pole alongside your cockatiel so it can hop onto its super-long perch. When you have lowered the pole, you can ask the cockatiel to hop onto your hand.

A long pole can be used as an extended perch if your cockatiel is out of reach.

- When you are getting a quick and consistent response, wait before rewarding your cockatiel. The bird will be expecting a treat and will try to work out how to get it. In most cases, the bird will come closer to you. Immediately reward your cockatiel with a treat.
- Build up this exercise in easy stages until the cockatiel realizes that it will not get a treat until it comes and perches on your hand. Tiels are quick learners, so it will not be long before you have a perfect cockatiel recall!

HAPPY LANDINGS

A cockatiel that is confident with people is happy to perch on a head, an arm, or a shoulder. With the larger species of Parrots, this is not to be encouraged. A large Parrot beak could inflict serious injury, and it is therefore inadvisable to allow the Parrot near to your face.

However, if you have a tame tiel that never tries to bite, you can train it to land on your head or your shoulder. Place your hand on your head or shoulder, and, if the cockatiel is hand-trained, it will fly to your hand. It is then an easy matter to remove your hand. Think carefully before teaching your cockatiel this trick, as you may tire of it more quickly than the bird does. If you have young children, it is better that your cockatiels never get into the habit of perching on any part of the body except the hand.

HOUSE-TRAINING

Cleaning up after your cockatiel is a job that every bird keeper must take on. Cages and aviaries need routine care to keep them clean and hygienic. However, you can reduce the workload by house-training your tiel when it is spending time outside its cage. This is easy to achieve, and means you will probably allow your cockatiel more free-flying time if you do not have to clean up droppings.

A tame cockatiel will be happy to perch on your shoulder.

Due to the nature of their diet, and the fact that flying birds must be as light as possible, cockatiels defecate quite frequently. The largest droppings will be eliminated when the bird awakens after spending the night roosting. Use this knowledge to house-train your cockatiel.

- As soon as you have removed the cage cover in the morning, take the cockatiel to its playstand. The playstand comes with a tray to catch droppings. You can make this more effective by lining the tray with newspaper.
- When your cockatiel is on its playstand, wait until the bird has defecated. Then give lots of praise, showing how pleased you are with your tiel's behavior. You could even produce a favorite toy and have a game.
- Leave your cockatiel for 20 minutes or so. When you return, take the bird back to its playstand. It will probably defecate again.

Reward your tiel with lots of praise.
- Keep repeating this routine, and, in time, your cockatiel will learn that when it wants to defecate, it must return to the playstand. Remember to praise your cockatiel every time it performs correctly. Do not make the mistake of admonishing your tiel if it makes a mistake. The cockatiel will not understand the cause of your anger. The bird may even become uncooperative, as it cannot "read" your behavior and will be wary of trusting you.

CLICKER TRAINING

If you want to extend your cockatiel's repertoire of tricks, you may consider clicker training. This is a method of training pioneered by Karen Pryor when she was working with dolphins. She developed a system that is now used with great success on a range of animals, including birds.

A clicker is a matchbox-shaped box with a metal tongue that "clicks" when you press it. The click is a "yes" marker that signals the precise moment the cockatiel has carried out a correct behavior. The bird is then rewarded with a treat. The bird soon associates the sound of a click with getting a reward and therefore tries to earn a click by producing the behavior you want.

The great beauty of clicker training is that it ends all confusion between bird and trainer. It is all too easy to send out mixed messages, rewarding the cockatiel after it has performed a trick rather than when it is doing what you want. The bird does not understand what it is being rewarded for, and is therefore unlikely to repeat the behavior. With a clicker, you can "click" the instant that your cockatiel produces the behavior you want. The bird will grow in confidence and will be ready to repeat the behavior, as it knows that a reward will follow.

Cockatiels are intelligent birds and are quick to catch onto the concept of clicker training.

Getting started

The first objective is to teach your cockatiel what a click means. Choose a time when your tiel is bright and alert, and has not recently eaten. Prepare some treats, such as sunflower seeds, that your cockatiel will want to work for. It is important to keep the treats small; if they take too long to eat, the training session will be ruined by interruptions.

• Arm yourself with a bowl of treats and a clicker. Hold out your hand, and as soon as the cockatiel steps onto it, click and reward. At this stage of training, you can click any behavior, such as the bird looking at you when you call its name. The aim is to establish the link between response, click, and reward.

• Repeat the exercise, clicking and rewarding when your tiel responds. Within a matter of minutes, the cockatiel will learn that the click means *"okay,"* and a treat will follow.

• When you are confident that your cockatiel is responding consistently, add a command, such as *"Up"* if it is stepping onto your hand, or *"Watch"* if your tiel is turning to look at you.

TRICK TRAINING

Once your cockatiel understands what a click means, it will start working to earn one. This is when your training will take off, as the bird knows it must perform a behavior in order to win a treat.

Remember, each training session should be short—no more than five minutes maximum. Start with a relatively straightforward exercise, such as climbing a ladder.

- Prepare a bowl of treats, and place your finger on the bottom rung of the ladder. If your cockatiel is hand-trained, it will hop onto the ladder. Click and reward.

With practice, you can train your cockatiel to climb up a ladder or a rope on command.

- Cockatiels are great mimics, so all you have to do is use your finger to "climb" up the ladder. The tiel will follow your fingers and move onto the next rung of the ladder. Click and reward.
- Keep repeating the exercise, clicking and rewarding until your cockatiel understands what is required. Then add a word of command, such as "*Climb.*"
- Each time, make the tiel work a little harder before you click. The cockatiel will learn that it must keep on climbing before it earns a click.
- With practice, your cockatiel will respond to the command, and will climb all the way up the ladder, knowing it will get a click and a reward when it completes the exercise.

Once you and your cockatiel have mastered the art of clicker training, there will be no stopping you. You can train your tiel to fly to a chosen object, fly from one person to another, ring a bell, or even lift up one foot at a time! The secret is to break down each trick into simple stages. Click and reward at each stage, and only move onto the next stage when you are confident that your cockatiel understands what is required. The final stage is adding the verbal command, and then clicking and rewarding the cockatiel only when it has performed the trick.

VOICE TRAINING

Like all members of the Parrot family, cockatiels are vocal birds. They love to use their voices and will be delighted to join in voice training sessions. Natural mimics, cockatiels can learn to copy sounds. This may be simply repeating the chattering or cooing sound you make when you are talking to your cockatiels. Some cockatiels copy household noises, such as the phone ringing, or you can train your cockatiel to repeat words and whistle tunes.

Cockatiels are not the greatest talkers of the Parrot family, but they can be taught a number of different words, or they can be trained to put a couple of words together. Whistling comes naturally, and many tiels have been taught to whistle a favorite tune. There is no doubt that some cockatiels are better talkers and singers than others. Generally, cocks are more proficient, as they use their voices when they are attracting hens. But if a cockatiel has bonded closely with its owner, it will generally take to voice training.

As well as assessing the attributes of the cockatiel when it comes to voice training, you also need to evaluate your own role. Many aspects of bird keeping involve a high degree of patience, but none more so than voice training. The more time and patience you have, the better the results will be.

Getting started

Choose a time when your cockatiel is alert and active, and make sure the room where you are training is quiet and free from distractions. Do not attempt voice training if other tiels are within hearing distance, as your student

A cock (pictured right) will be a better talker than a hen (left).

cockatiel will be too busy talking to the other cockatiels to concentrate on you.

- Choose a word, and speak with a bright, lively voice. Wait a moment to give the cockatiel a chance to absorb the word.
- Repeat the word, using exactly the same tone of voice. Initially, your cockatiel may not attempt to repeat the word, but don't be put off. Break off before your bird loses interest.
- The following day, repeat the lesson. This time, you are far more likely to get a response. If the tiel makes a sound that resembles the word, you should immediately reward its efforts.

• Some bird keepers recommend teaching a bird when the cover is on its cage. Obviously this means the cockatiel has no distractions and will focus completely on your voice.

It will take many lessons before your cockatiel masters a word, but, once learned, the word will never be forgotten. In fact, your tiel will delight in repeating it at every available opportunity!

When your cockatiel has learned one word, add to its vocabulary by teaching it additional words. You can try stringing a couple of words together to make a short phrase, but this takes longer to teach and has to be trained in stages, a word at a time.

Some cockatiels seem to prefer whistling to talking. If you want to train your cockatiel to

TIME FOR FLAPPIES

Nicole Johnson from Minnesota first lost her heart to a cockatiel at the tender age of 12, when her aunt's pet bird would sing to her while she fed it crackers. Today, Nicole's family consists of one husband, two children, three cats, and 11 cockatiels. Nicole has taught a repertoire of tricks to her feathered friends. "Cockatiels are delightful creatures, affectionate and highly intelligent. Some learn to talk, although they are not known for their extensive vocabularies. The only two words my male tiels know are 'birdy' and 'pretty birdy' and not everyone who hears them understands them. They are, however, excellent at mimicking sounds and whistling. They can mimic the sound of a wild robin, the telephone, and some

Taxi performs flappies on owner Nicole's hand.

tunes from video games, and many other cockatiel owners I know have similar stories.

"Rather than concentrating on talk training, I have enjoyed teaching tricks to my tiels. One of the first tricks I ever taught was to my male tiel, Neo. I taught him 'flappies' on command. This is where I say, 'Neo, do flappies' and then Neo stands on the end of his perch and flaps his wings vigorously for several seconds. This is quite a simple trick to teach. When Neo flapped his wings for exercise, I'd call out 'flappies' and flap my hands with him. It wasn't long before Neo attached the meaning of the word with the action. When I said 'flappies' he began to do the action by himself, to show me that he knew what I was repeat a tune, simply play the music time and time again. Repetition is the key to success. Cockatiels do not have a voice box and vocal cords as we do. Instead, they produce sounds through the syrinx, which is a complex structure made up of muscles and membranes. Small muscles control variations in sound, which gives the bird great versatility. Some cockatiels can even whistle two tunes at the same time.

If you do not have the time to spend voice training your cockatiel, you can buy a parrot training CD, which is specially designed to teach birds to talk. There are also music CDs with tunes that your cockatiel will be able to learn. Obviously you miss out on the personal interaction, and the satisfaction of teaching the bird yourself, but the CDs do work, and your cockatiel will become a hugely entertaining pet.

saying. I instantly rewarded him with praise and made a big deal out of it. I've now taught 'flappies' to one of my other tiels, Taxi, as well.

"Neo is my star performer. We have a little routine where I say to him, 'Are you a birdy?' and Neo responds by nodding his head. But I've taught tricks to my other tiels as well. At the moment, I'm working on clicker training with my baby cockatiels, so that they will fly to me when I click. That's quite a lot of fun. I've also taught my hen, Apache, to play basketball, and Buzz, my newly adopted whiteface male, sings for his supper.

"Cockatiels are clever birds and they need a lot of mental stimulation, so trick training is an ideal pastime for them. But it's very important to establish a trusting relationship first. You won't get far, otherwise! The secret to success is to keep it simple. Start out with something the bird does naturally and build on it with praise and encouragement. Watch your bird closely, and you'll soon notice certain behaviors that your tiel enjoys and repeats regularly. Put a name to them and encourage your bird to do them on command—just

as I did with 'flappies'. Always remember to reward your bird when it has done what you want. The three golden rules of trick training are repetition, praise, and consistency.

"It is very important that you never try to force a bird to learn a trick. He has to *want* to do what you ask. Some birds can 'unlearn' tricks, or choose to perform them only when *they* feel like it. But even if your pet is

Apache slams one in the net!

being uncooperative, you should never punish it. Instead you need to work harder on the reward. Most cockatiels in a happy home are quite eager to please, so regular training and plenty of praise will result in most birds remembering their tricks."

CHAPTER NINE

TROUBLESHOOTING

Cockatiels adapt very well to a life in captivity, and, if they are cared for properly, they will be completely contented. A captive bird does not yearn for a freedom it has never known and will be perfectly happy with its home-based existence.

Problems will occur only if you are failing to cater for your tiel's needs, or if your bird's behavior has gone uncorrected and the cockatiel has not learned its place in the family flock.

PECKING ORDER

As we have seen, cockatiels accept the concept of leadership, and it is unlikely that a bird will attempt to become dominant provided you give clear guidelines as to what constitutes acceptable behavior.

Hopefully, the breeder will have gotten training off to a good start and laid some ground rules firmly in place. Your job is to continue with this work as your cockatiel matures.

Golden rules

If you stick to the following rules, your tiel will understand its place in the family pecking order and will accept your leadership:

- Do not respond to your cockatiel when it is using its voice to get your attention. A cockatiel must learn that this behavior is unrewarding; it does not produce results, so there is no point continuing with it.
- Do not allow your tiel to nibble your fingers. A cockatiel must learn that it never uses its beak when it is interacting with people.
- Always invite your cockatiel to come to you, rather than letting the bird make up its own mind. A bird that is allowed to fly at you and land on your head, whether you like it or not, is controlling the situation. A tiel should respect your personal space.
- Work at hand-training and recall, so you do not have to battle with your cockatiel when it has to return to its cage.

• Handle your cockatiel on a regular basis, so that it will accept all care procedures without protest.

There are also a number of rules you should obey to ensure your cockatiel is being treated with kindness and with respect.

• Be patient—the first rule for all bird keepers! Even if a cockatiel is trying your patience by delaying the moment it returns to its cage, never lose your temper or attempt to grab the bird. Tiels are easily scared and will quickly decide that you are not to be trusted.

You can have a close and rewarding relationship with a cockatiel, as long as it understands that you are at the top of the pecking order.

• Be tactful when disturbing caged cockatiels. You are entering their personal space and you should make the intervention as low key as possible. Do not make sudden movements or loud noises that will frighten the birds.

• Provide suitable companionship. If you are keeping a single bird, you must find the time to be your tiel's friend and companion. If you have a number of cockatiels, make sure the cage does not become overcrowded, or there may be an outbreak of bullying.

• Establish a routine so that your cockatiel knows when it is feeding time, when it is allowed out of its cage, and when it is bedtime. A tiel will be much happier if it knows the order of events rather than wondering when you are going to appear with food, or fretting because it does not know when it is going to be released from its cage.

KEY STAGES

There are a couple of trying times during a cockatiel's life when behavior may change. If you have a happy, well-trained tiel, any difficulties you experience will be of only a temporary nature.

Adolescence

Sometimes a cockatiel will go through a problem phase when it is hitting adolescence. A bird that has previously been well behaved can start having teenage tantrums, screaming, nipping, or becoming hugely attention-seeking. This is only a temporary state of affairs, and, as long as you are firm and consistent with your handling, the cockatiel will return to its former good manners. Do not give in to your tiel during this phase, or it will start to believe that it can be the leader.

Breeding condition

Behavior may change when an adult bird comes into breeding condition, which is at around 18 months of age. This usually happens in the spring, and is triggered by longer daylight hours. Even if you are not keeping tiels for breeding, you will still see marked changes in your birds at this time.

A hen may become preoccupied with nest making, and if she does not have a male companion, she may start to lay unfertilized eggs. Do not attempt to remove the eggs. The hen will only try to lay more, and she may become seriously weakened from the effort. A hen has a strong urge to protect her eggs and could resent too much interference with the cage at this time. Another sign of protectiveness is when a hen hangs upside down on the cage door, with her wings spread wide like a bat. This looks quite comical, but in fact the hen is protecting the entrance to the cage in exactly the same way that a wild bird would protect the entrance to her nest.

When a cock is in breeding condition, he may become aggressive. This type of behavior is far more likely to be a problem if you are keeping a single bird that has no outlet for natural behavior. A lone cock that is strongly bonded to its keeper may also display courtship behavior,

You may see a distinct change in behavior when a cock is in breeding condition.

thinking of its primary companion as its mate. A bird may regurgitate on its keeper, or it may even try to mate the keeper's hand. If this happens, do not become angry or upset; your cockatiel is only doing what comes naturally. Keep to your normal routine, but try not to overhandle your tiel at this time.

PROBLEM BEHAVIORS

Despite the best of intentions, things can go wrong and a cockatiel may develop behavioral problems that cannot be attributed to hormonal changes. It may be that you have taken on an older bird that is having trouble adapting to its new home; you may have a cockatiel that has not been sufficiently handled as a chick and is wary of its human family; or you may have a single bird that has bonded too closely with you.

Overbonding

This can occur when a cockatiel is kept alone. If you choose to keep a single bird, you have the advantage of owning a tame bird that interacts very closely with you. But the disadvantage is that the bird relies on you for everything. You are leader, carer, companion, and mate, which is a tall order for anyone! You must be prepared to become the primary companion and give your tiel the time it needs. You can devise training programs and invent games to keep your cockatiel mentally stimulated. You can handle your cockatiel regularly, petting it and stroking it, and you can allow the cockatiel lots of free time outside its cage. But despite your best efforts, a single cockatiel may still develop

A cockatiel may become highly attention seeking if it has overbonded with its owner.

behavioral problems simply because it has become too dependent on one person. This behavior can take different forms, but may include the following:

• Screaming or squawking for attention.
• Refusing to be handled by anyone except its primary companion.
• Directing courtship behavior toward its primary companion.
• Becoming jealous if other people interact with the primary companion.
• Refusing to eat and becoming depressed if the primary companion is absent. In severe cases, the cockatiel may pluck its feathers (see page 99).

Solutions

The simple and obvious solution is to get another cockatiel. This may well be in the bird's best interests and should be seriously considered. However, you need to bear in mind that if a certain behavior has become a habit, your cockatiel may not give up the behavior even though the reason for it has gone.

There are a number of steps you can take to make your cockatiel less dependent on you. These include the following:

• Train your tiel to go to other people. This will take time, and you need to supervise all interactions. Make sure the "stranger" has lots of treats, and do not try to rush the cockatiel into changing allegiance. In time, the cockatiel will be attracted by the treats and will start learning that it can trust other people.

- Accustom your cockatiel to time alone. Ignore demands for attention, and only reward your tiel when it is quiet.
- Rotate toys so the cockatiel has new things to play with. Shredding toys, such as a paperback, will provide plenty of occupation.

Biting

A cockatiel uses its beak to explore and investigate its surroundings. It is natural for a cockatiel to gnaw and shred, but the beak should never be used aggressively. Cockatiels do not bite each other in the wild. If a bird wants to exert its authority over another bird, it uses threatening body language rather than resorting to physical violence. If your cockatiel starts biting you, you need to discover the underlying cause.

A cockatiel may bite for the following reasons:

- A chick's exploratory nibbling has not been checked, and the bird has got into the habit of biting its human family.
- A cockatiel is going through temporary hormonal changes (see Adolescence, Breeding Condition).
- You have not established yourself as leader, and the cockatiel is challenging your authority.
- The cockatiel has been traumatized by a bad handling experience, such as poor wing clipping, and has taken a dislike to people.
- The cockatiel has not had sufficient handling while it was growing up.
- A cockatiel may bite out of jealousy, if it has bonded too closely with its human companion.

It may help if you have some form of protection when you are training your cockatiel not to bite.

- The cockatiel may have become overprotective about its cage or playstand.
- A training session has gone on too long, and the tiel has become overtired or frustrated.

If your cockatiel has no history of biting and the problem develops out of the blue, it is advisable to make an appointment with an avian veterinarian. There may be a physical reason for your tiel's change of behavior.

Solutions

There are a number of ways to stop a bird from biting once you have discovered the reason for the behavior.

- If a chick is using its beak too freely, it must be discouraged. Say "*No*" in a firm tone of voice, and give the chick a really fierce look. Cockatiels read facial expressions very

If you have a lone cockatiel that screams, you may solve the problem by getting a companion bird.

accurately and the bird will understand that its behavior is undesirable.

- Work on handling exercises, such as getting the cockatiel to step on and off your hand, to establish your leadership. Do not allow the cockatiel to perch on your head, as the bird will believe it is superior.
- It will take time and patience to tame a cockatiel that has not been used to handling or has had a bad experience. You can try wearing gloves or wrapping your finger in a towel, so that you can pet your cockatiel. If it tries to bite, you are protected, and you can simply ignore the undesirable behavior. Make sure you have lots of treats so you can reward your cockatiel when it is tolerating being touched without attempting to bite. In time, the cockatiel will see that there is nothing to fear and will stop biting.

- If a tiel is biting out of jealousy, you need to supervise and increase interactions with other members of the family so the bird does not become too focused on one person.
- If your cockatiel tries to bite because it is protecting its cage, return to the early stages of training when the bird was taught to step on and off your hand on command. If necessary, use a small wooden perch, rather than your hand. Retraining the exercise will teach your cockatiel to respect your authority so that it stops trying to take control.
- Never prolong training sessions, even if you have not achieved your goal. In fact, if a cockatiel is not in the mood for training, it is better to give it a miss and try again later. Training should always be positive.

Screaming

Cockatiels like to use their voices, and noise levels can rise, particularly at dawn and at dusk. In fact, cockatiels are one of the quieter members of the Parrot family, so it is rare for calling to become a major problem. If a tiel is indulging in prolonged bouts of screaming, there could be a number reasons why:

- The cockatiel may be attention-seeking (more likely to happen to a bird kept alone).
- The cage may be in a noisy room, with a television or stereo blaring. In this situation, a tiel may be mimicking or competing with the sounds it hears.

- A cockatiel may compete with its cage companion to see who can be the loudest.
- Breeding condition can prompt an increase in noise levels.
- The cockatiel may be bored and frustrated, particularly if left in its cage for long periods.
- The cage may be too small, or overcrowded with toys and other equipment.
- The cockatiel may not be getting enough rest (see page 100) and is stressed and overtired.

As with other problems, seek the advice of an avian veterinarian to make sure there is no underlying physical reason for your cockatiel's behavior.

Solutions

If you have a lone cockatiel, consider getting a companion. This will relieve boredom and, hopefully, put a stop to attention-seeking behavior. You can also try working on some training exercises to assert your authority if you think your tiel has become undisciplined.

Making changes in your bird's living conditions may well solve the problem of screaming.

- Check out the cage, and make sure your cockatiels have enough space.
- Place the cage in a quiet room.
- Do not reward your cockatiel by shouting at the bird and telling it to stop every time it screams. Reward the cockatiel when it is quiet and ignore it when it screams.
- Buy a cover for the cage so the cockatiel gets sufficient rest.

TRAINING AIDS

If you have clicker trained your cockatiel (see page 86), you can use this training aid to correct behavior as well as to teach new exercises. When your tiel is behaving inappropriately, ignore it completely. When the bird stops the inappropriate behavior, be quick to reward with a click and a treat. The cockatiel will soon learn what behavior reaps rewards.

- Give your cockatiel more time out of its cage, and increase the bird's mental stimulation with new toys and training exercises.

Feather plucking

This is a distressing condition where the cockatiel plucks at its own feathers until it becomes bald. The areas most often affected are the chest and the legs, which can become very sore. Feather plucking is very different from normal preening where some feather loss is expected, particularly when the bird is molting. Abnormal feather plucking can be seen as overzealous preening, where the bird will actually harm itself. This is a condition that is seen only in captive birds. There are a number of reasons why a bird may resort to this type of behavior:

Medical: There are a number of medical causes for feather plucking, including the presence of

A tired or stressed cockatiel may resort to plucking its feathers.

mites, an allergy, an infection, or liver disease.

Poisoning: Poisonous residues of lead or zinc on poor-quality cage wire, ingested by the tiel, have been known to trigger feather plucking.

Dietary: An unbalanced diet, where seed is the main food and there is a lack of fresh fruit and vegetables, can cause feather plucking.

If a tiel starts feather plucking, the first step is to take it to an avian veterinarian who will find out if there is a medical or dietary cause. If the cockatiel is pronounced fit and well, you will need to examine the environment that your cockatiel is living in, and try to discover what is upsetting the bird. There are a number of reasons why a cockatiel may become obsessed with plucking its own feathers and self-harming:

• Boredom and frustration: Often the result of being confined in a cage for long periods.

• Loneliness: Cockatiels that are denied companionship—human or avian—may resort to feather plucking.

• Sexual frustration: This can occur in the breeding season if a cockatiel does not have a breeding partner.

• Attention-seeking: This is more likely to occur in cases of overbonding.

• Insecurity: A cockatiel has not received consistent training and has become stressed and confused.

• The need to bathe: Normal preening can occur only if a cockatiel has access to fresh, clean water. If this is not available, the bird may become so uncomfortable that it plucks its feathers rather than preen them.

• Poor wing clipping: If the wings are clipped so severely that a cockatiel is deprived of flight, or is unbalanced and cannot fly properly, it will become very distressed and may start feather plucking.

• Stress: Cockatiels are sensitive birds and may become worried by change. This could include going to a new home, or the cockatiel may become fearful of something new in its cage or in the room where it lives.

If your cockatiel keeps plucking its feathers, try spraying it with diluted aloe vera. This natural remedy has a very soothing effect and also encourages the re-growth of feathers.

- Fatigue: Tiels need to rest, and if they are in a noisy room where the lights are always blazing, the bird will become stressed through exhaustion.

Solutions

If feather plucking has an environmental cause, you will need to take steps to change the way you are keeping your cockatiel. Try the following suggestions:

- Spend time with your cockatiel so that it feels safe and secure with you, and accepts you as its leader.
- Ensure that your cockatiel has free-flying periods outside the cage every day.
- Provide mental stimulation in the form of new toys, teaching your cockatiel tricks and adding variety to its diet.
- Try not to reward the attention-seeking cockatiel by shouting at it every time you see it feather plucking. Say "*No*" in a very firm voice and then ignore it completely. The moment the cockatiel stops feather plucking, go to the cage/perch and reward the bird with lots of praise and maybe a treat. In this way, you are rewarding the bird for the behavior you want.
- Make sure your tiel has water for bathing, or spray the bird two or three times a week.
- Clipped feathers do regrow, so if poor wing clipping is a possible cause, a cockatiel will regain its flying ability in time and will hopefully stop plucking its feathers. But take warning from what has happened, and seek expert advice before attempting to clip the feathers on subsequent occasions.

Provide mental stimulation in the form of new toys.

- If you have a lone cockatiel, consider getting a companion bird or a breeding partner.

One of the worst problems with feather plucking is that it can become a habit that is very difficult to break, even if you have removed the underlying reason for the behavior. If this happens, you will need to be patient and work at ignoring the cockatiel when it is feather plucking, and rewarding it when it stops. Eventually, the tiel will learn that feather plucking is a totally nonproductive type of behavior.

Night frights

This is when a cockatiel is suddenly disturbed at night and goes into a panic. The bird will attempt to escape from the supposed danger, and will thrash around its cage, risking severe injury. The underlying reason for night frights is that cockatiels see very poorly in the dark. If a cockatiel is disturbed from sleep, it fails to get its bearings and becomes increasingly distressed and frightened. This is often exacerbated by the cockatiel flying into toys in the cage.

If your cockatiel experiences night frights, put the lights on immediately. Go to the cage, and

---

SCREAMING EBO

Screaming is a fairly common problem, but it needn't drive owners to distraction, as Shobana Appavu, loving owner of Ebo, testifies.

"I've had Ebo for about two-and-a-half years," says Shobana. "As a younger bird, Ebo was incredibly clingy. All he wanted was to be right by my side, which sounds really cute but isn't always practical. Whenever I left the room, he'd scream constantly until I came back. If I was out of the room for 10 minutes, he'd yell for the entire 10 minutes.

"In the beginning, when Ebo yelled, I scolded him by saying 'Ebo!' in an angry voice. Of course, this didn't change his behavior at all. Ebo likes to vocalize in plenty of ways, including speaking, singing, and whistling. Instead of stopping screaming, he just started yelling and then scolding himself in an angry voice. It was actually pretty amusing.

"Having realized that scolding Ebo was getting me nowhere, I read up about screaming. Over the course of a year or so, I tried plenty of techniques I'd read about in books or online. Mostly I just ignored it, so that I didn't accidentally reinforce his behavior by paying attention to him when he screamed.

"The solution really came about by accident. Just before I got Ebo he'd had a horrible wing clip that made him hurtle backward and land on his tail whenever he tried to take off. He couldn't go anywhere unless I put him there. After his first molt, I decided that I would let Ebo stay flighted. Once his feathers grew back, it wasn't long before he realized that if I walked across the room, he could fly after me. In the beginning he flew after me all the time. When I didn't want him to follow me, I'd just launch him back to his play gym. Basically, I was trying to encourage him to be more independent. Now if Ebo tries to fly after me and I don't want him landing on me, all I have to do is hold up my arm and he'll fly back to his gym.

"Anyway, with this development I suddenly noticed that Ebo's yelling had decreased dramatically. I think he was yelling because he felt talk in a soft, reassuring voice. Do not attempt to open the cage door or grab the bird until it has had a chance to settle and calm down.

Solutions

There are a number of steps you can take that will minimize the risk of night frights:

- Leave a dim light on in the room where your cockatiels are kept.

- At night, do not allow anyone to enter the room where your cockatiels are kept.
- If you are using a cage cover, leave part of the cage uncovered so the cockatiels are not left in complete darkness.
- Leave the radio on (making sure you are on a channel that plays soft, soothing music). You can even buy CDs especially made for captive birds; they feature sounds taken from the wild that will help your birds to relax.

very vulnerable when he couldn't fly and was left alone. Once he was fully flighted, he was no longer as dependent on me and he felt more secure. There was no definite moment when I realized we'd solved the problem; it was a gradual shift in his behavior that I didn't notice until I looked back on how it used to be.

"It's a relief to have Ebo's screaming under control, but it will never be eliminated completely. Screaming is totally natural behavior for a cockatiel and it wouldn't be reasonable for me to expect him to stop completely. I've learned that I really had to meet Ebo halfway. I had to gain that extra bit of patience and tolerance with him and just get used to it. That's an important point to bear in mind when dealing with any behavioral problem. You must learn to tell the difference between a cockatiel that has a real problem behavior, and a cockatiel that is exhibiting completely natural—albeit annoying— behavior. Most 'problem' behavior makes perfect sense when seen from the cockatiel's point of view. If it's natural behavior, the human is the one

who needs to change.

"Ebo will never be a quiet bird. Sometimes his special Ebo songs can get really loud and distracting. But obviously, I don't want to discourage that too much, because it's cute and that's Ebo!"

With a lot of patience and understanding from his owner, Ebo has now become a quieter member of the family.

CHAPTER TEN

BREEDING AND EXHIBITING COCKATIELS

Keeping cockatiels is a hobby that grows on you. There are lots of stories of people who have started out with one bird and have gone onto establish a breeding program and then become involved in showing top-quality cockatiels.

You may feel that keeping pet cockatiels is all you want to do, but it is still interesting to find out about the breeding habits of cockatiels, and to discover what goes on in the show world. Here is a brief overview that will give you an idea of what is involved in breeding and showing cockatiels.

BREEDING BASICS

Cockatiels are relatively easy birds to breed, but you should think very carefully before pursuing this aspect of bird keeping. There are a number of important considerations before you decide to go ahead.

Time: Breeding cockatiels is very rewarding, but it is time-consuming, requiring both dedication and patience. This is particularly true when you are rearing the young chicks so that they become used to being handled by people.

Money: You need to provide suitable accommodations and the correct diet for breeding birds and chicks. It could well be that you do not make any money from selling the chicks. As such, breeding should always be considered as a hobby rather than an investment.

Veterinary care: Of course, you hope that there will be no problems with the hen or her chicks, but if problems arise, you must be prepared to enlist the help of an avian veterinarian without delay.

Finding homes: If you have limited space, you will need to find homes for the chicks by the time they are seven to eight weeks old.

Lifelong responsibility: You also want to be confident that the tiels you breed go to homes where they will receive the best possible care. If you are a cockatiel breeder, you are responsible for every bird that is bred under your care. If necessary, you should be prepared to take a bird back if its home proves to be unsuitable.

Pet or show: You need to decide whether you are breeding cockatiels purely as pets, or whether you want to get involved in breeding and producing show-quality birds. There is an argument that says you should always attempt to produce top-quality birds for the good of the species, but breeding show birds does require additional knowledge and experience.

GETTING STARTED

If, after due consideration, you are anxious to get involved in breeding cockatiels, the best plan is to do your homework. Read as much as possible about breeding and showing cockatiels, and spend time on the Internet, researching cockatiel Web sites. It is also useful to consult with breeders, as you will derive great benefit from their practical experience, which may have been built up over many years.

When you have gathered as much information as possible, you will be ready to plan a breeding program.

A BREEDING PAIR

Although it may sound obvious, the first step is ensuring that you have a cock and a hen. Tiels that live together bond very closely and may appear like a mated pair even when they are the same sex. There are a number of ways to check the sex of your birds:

- For most color varieties, you can determine the sex once the birds have molted into their adult plumage at around six months of age. However, the pied varieties are notoriously difficult to sex.
- You can pluck three or four feathers from your cockatiel's breast, and send them to a DNA testing laboratory (your avian veterinarian will have contact details). The result is usually available in a week.
- Clip a nail a little too short to produce a few drops of blood, which can be sent for DNA testing. This method means that even a featherless chick can be correctly sexed.

It is advisable to wait until cockatiels are 18 months of age before starting a breeding program.

- Tiels can be surgically sexed, which involves a vet anesthetizing the cockatiel so it can be examined internally. Obviously, putting a cockatiel under an anesthetic involves a certain amount of risk.

The right age
The best chance of producing healthy chicks is to breed cockatiels that are at least 18 months of age. Cocks that are younger may be infertile; hens may suffer from physical complications, such as egg binding (see page 125).

Health and well-being
Breeding cockatiels should be fit, healthy, and in tip-top condition. This is particularly applicable to hens, as producing eggs is an energy-sapping business. Obesity is a particular problem, as an obese hen may be prone to egg binding. For information on health conditions relating to breeding, see page 125.

Bloodlines
When you are planning a breeding program, try to ensure that your birds are not related, or not too closely related. Inbreeding (such as breeding a mother to a son, or a father to a daughter) can produce a variety of problems. Chicks can be born with defects, such as missing toes, and they are generally more susceptible to disease.

Color varieties
The science of breeding for color is highly complex, and you will need to spend time researching pedigrees and choosing breeding partners in order to produce recognized color varieties.

If introductions are supervised, it will not take long before the cock and hen bond with each other.

Show quality
If you are planning to get involved in showing cockatiels, it is essential that you find breeding stock that is of show quality. You will need to go to a special breeder for cockatiels of this caliber, and you will have to pay more for them.

Introductions
If you have bought a cock and a hen especially for breeding, rather than breeding with cockatiels that already live together, you will have to supervise an introductory period where the two birds get to know each other. Use the same method as when introducing companion birds (see page 43). Place two cages next to each other, making sure you leave a gap between the cages in case the cockatiels try to bite each other. Over a period of a few days, observe the cockatiels' behavior. Hopefully, they will start to perch closer to each other, so you can try moving the cages a little closer, keeping a check on the birds' reactions. With luck, it will be a case of love at first sight, and you can move the

cockatiels in together within a week. Sometimes a pair will take longer to bond, and it may be advisable to wait a couple of weeks. If, after a month, the birds appear indifferent or even aggressive, you would be advised to try a different pairing.

READY TO BREED

The breeding season coincides with longer hours of daylight between the spring and the fall. A healthy, well-balanced diet and frequent bathing or spraying will help to trigger the process. Some aviculturists feed specially manufactured breeder's pellets, which have an increased level of protein, as a way of encouraging readiness to breed.

In most cases, it is the introduction of a nest box that sets the cockatiels on the right track. The nest box should be 12 to 15 inches (30.5 to 38 cm) in height, and 9–12 inches (23–30.5 cm) square. The entrance, which should be 3 inches (7.5 cm) in diameter, should be placed a few inches below the top of the box, and slightly to one side of center. There should be a perch alongside the entrance hole. In most cases, there is a hinged inspection door at the roof of the box.

The floor of the nest box should be lined with nesting material. This is a matter of choice, but shredded paper towels work well. Some bird keepers prefer to use peat or shavings. Never use pine or cedar shavings, as they could be very harmful. They release phenols when damp, which can have an adverse effect on a bird's respiratory system. When you arrange the nesting material, make a small dent in the middle. This is known as the nest bowl, and it helps to prevent the eggs from rolling out of the nest area.

While the cockatiels are getting used to their nest box, it is a good idea if you accustom them to regular checks, using the inspection door. If the birds are familiar with this disturbance, they will not be alarmed when you use the inspection door to check them when they are incubating eggs or when the chicks hatch.

INCUBATION

Eggs are laid seven to ten days after mating. A hen cockatiel will lay four to six eggs, on alternate days. Clutches with up to eight eggs are not unknown, but it is unlikely that all the eggs will hatch. Eggs laid on the bottom of the cage floor will rarely hatch, although you can try putting them in nesting material in the hope that the parents will start sitting on them. It is important that the eggs are kept as still as possible. If an egg rolls out of the nest, or is suddenly jolted by an adult bird, it may become addled. This means that the contents of the egg are shaken up, and the embryos may be destroyed so that the eggs will not hatch.

You can inspect the eggs that are laid by using a candler. This is a flashlightlike instrument that is used to illuminate an egg in order to spot any imperfections in the shell or in the contents of the egg. After five days, you can use the candler to see if there is a faint red circle within the yolk of the egg. This is the first stage of growth. It will be followed by a red blob appearing within the circle, which is the embryo, and then veins start to radiate from it. As the embryo develops,

HATCHING AND REARING

Eggs are laid on alternate days.

The cock and hen share incubation duties.

The first chick hatches.

A day-old chick.

The same chick, now 11 days old.

The wing feathers are starting to grow.

At 15 days, the chick's plumage is growing fast.

At 29 days, the crest is developing.

the veins occupy more and more of the egg until they cover all of it, with the exception of the air space. This is the gap located at the blunt end of the egg at the end of incubation.

The process of incubating the eggs does not start until two or three eggs have been laid. Both the cock and the hen are involved in incubating, often dividing duties so the hen sits on the eggs at night, and the cock takes over during the day. Sometimes both birds will sit on the nest together.

It is important to provide a bowl of water so that the adult birds can wet their feathers before sitting on the eggs. This helps to maintain the correct level of humidity. Adult birds will also turn the eggs, often on a regular, hourly basis during the day. This is to prevent the chick from sticking to the side of the shell and to allow for correct development.

HATCHING

The incubation period lasts between 18 and 21 days and then the eggs will hatch. A chick has an egg tooth, which is used to crack the eggshell, and it works its way around the circumference of the egg. The chick will push its back against the shell and then push its feet to the opposite side in order to break open the shell.

The chick is born wet, its eyes are closed, and it has yellow down on its body (or white down if it is a whiteface chick). The wings are only small buds.

For the first few hours of life, the chick needs warmth in order to dry out. The parents will not attempt to feed it until it is eight to twelve hours old and completely dry. Prior to this, the chick has obtained sufficient nourishment from absorbing the egg yolk before hatching out from the shell.

REARING THE CHICKS

The first meal the chicks receive from their parents is a very thin, liquid food, which is regurgitated from the crop. At this stage, the parents should be on a high-protein diet so they can cope with the chicks' demands. It is also helpful to feed soft food, which will be suitable for feeding the chicks. Hard-boiled egg is a good source of protein, but do not feed the egg whites. The albumin in the whites can accumulate to a toxic level in the parents. In addition to seed or pellets, other recommended food includes fresh corn, peas, carrots, broccoli, apples, bananas, pears, cooked pasta, and whole-wheat toast.

In the first few days, the chicks will sleep a lot and be fed by their parents. If a chick is too cold, it will shiver; if it is too hot, it will stick out its wings and pant. By the time a chick is eight days old, the eye slits will begin to open.

The body is still covered with yellow down, but, by 10 to 12 days, quills will be visible on the wings, and the crest will be starting to show. At this stage the eyes are fully open, and you will be able to see the opening to the ear. The chick will be able to hop about and beg for food. The chick's soft peep-peep call will change to louder, harsher cries for food.

Development is very swift, and, by 16 to 18 days, the wings are fully quilled and the tail quills are about half an inch (1 cm) in length. The yellow down gradually disappears and the chest, head, and body will be quilled by three weeks of age. At 26 to 28 days, the chicks will be fully feathered. Their wing feathers continue to grow, and the chicks will be ready to fledge when they are four to five weeks old.

EGG TIMER

The reason that there is a delay before the parents start incubating the eggs is so that all the eggs in a clutch will hatch at roughly the same time. An egg can be viable for up to seven days before it must be incubated.

Hand-feeding

If tiels are to live happily as captive birds, they need to get used to people from an early age. Generally, the parents will look after the chicks for the first 10 days, and, apart from regular checks, the breeder rarely plays an active role. Some breeders like to leave a radio playing near the nest box so that the chicks start to get used to human voices.

If a chick is left too long in the sole care of its parents, it will be completely wild and frightened of people. So, at around 10 days old, the chicks start learning the ways of humans. The easiest way to establish a positive relationship is to hand-feed the chicks. This is done using a sterile syringe, or a spoon, and dropping food into the chick's mouth. The chick soon learns that being held means being given food, and will be more than ready to accept the attention. Often a breeder will supplement natural feeding with a small proportion of hand-feeding in order that the chicks become tame.

As the chicks develop, they will start finding their own food. They should be feeding independently by the time they are four or five weeks old.

EXHIBITING COCKATIELS

As you learn more about cockatiels, you will start evaluating birds with a more critical eye, and you may want to try exhibiting quality cockatiels.

There are many cockatiel organizations operating in different countries, such as the American Cockatiel Society and the National Cockatiel Society in the United States, and the Cockatiel Society and the Scottish Cockatiel Association in the U.K.

These organizations promote the welfare of cockatiels, act as a forum of discussion and debate, serve as a registry, and also run shows. If you want to start showing cockatiels, the best plan is to contact these organizations or visit their Web sites (see page 128).

To begin with, it is worth going to a few cockatiel shows so that you can familiarize yourself with proceedings. The format of shows and judging procedures vary depending on the country where the show is being held and the host club. Generally, a club is affiliated to a national society, and the show will abide by the rules and regulations of that organization.

In most instances, there are a number of activities taking place on a show day. These include registrations, judging, and there is often a sales room where you can buy top-quality birds for your own breeding program. There are always lots of experienced aviculturists attending shows, so you will have the opportunity to talk to experts who will be able to give you valuable advice. The national organizations will have details of all show dates, or you can find out details in special bird magazines.

ENTERING A SHOW

When tiels are entered in a show, they are exhibited in a show cage. It is important that the cage meets the requirements of the governing body that is running the show, and judges will also take presentation and cleanliness into account when they make their evaluation. All cockatiels must be ringed, and exhibitors must produce proof of ownership.

Exhibiting cockatiels is a fascinating hobby that requires considerable dedication.

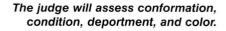

The judge will assess conformation, condition, deportment, and color.

Cockatiels are judged in classes depending on their color, and their age. Color divisions include the following: normal (grays), cinnamons, lutinos, pearls, pied, whitefaces. If rare colors, such as pastels, yellowfaces, or silvers are entered, the judge will decide on their classification. At some shows, there is a separate class for "rares."

JUDGING COCKATIELS

At a show, the cages are taken up to the judge's lighted bench, and each bird is evaluated according to the breed standard. This is a written description of the "perfect" cockatiel. Of course, there is no such thing as a perfect bird, but the judge's task is to look at each cockatiel and assess how closely it matches the standard. Each

organization has its own breed standard, which can vary slightly in detail. The judge will use the standard adopted by the club that is sponsoring the show.

The breed standard focuses on the following features:

- **General conformation:** This refers to size and body proportions. The body should be large in proportion, with a well-rounded chest and a broad shoulder span.
- **Detailed conformation:** This refers to the head, neck, wings, legs, and feet. The head should be large and round, ideally golf ball-shaped, placed on a strong neck. The wings should be carried naturally; a bird with

Points are awarded when cockatiels are placed on the top bench, which may vary depending on the size of the show and the number of entries. To win the title of Champion, a cockatiel must win at least 35 points, awarded by no fewer than three different judges. The cockatiel must also have one Best in Show award.

To become a Grand Champion, a cockatiel must win at least 75 points under four different judges. The cockatiel must also have one Best in Show award.

drooping shoulders will cross its wings tips, which is considered a fault. The legs should be long and strong, and the claws should be well kept and in proportion.

- **Condition:** This refers to the general condition of the bird, and its plumage in particular. The cockatiel should be clean, with good, tight feathers. Broken, frayed, or split feathers are faulted. Special attention should be paid to the wing and tail feathers, and the crest should have an upward sweep of approximately 40 mm.
- **Deportment:** This refers to a cockatiel's general demeanor, and its display on the show perch. The cockatiel should appear lively, and be happy to perch rather than remaining on the floor of the cage, or hugging the corners so it cannot be evaluated. The ideal stance is near upright, at a 70-degree angle from horizontal so that legs, feet, toes, and claws can be assessed.

- **Color:** The depth and uniformity of color should be judged. All colors and markings should be well defined, and clear plumage should not be interrupted by blotchiness. The head and face should be without blemish.

The judge will evaluate each cockatiel in turn, and will then make placings in each class. The best birds will be brought forward again in order to find the top placing overall, including a Best in Show.

SHOW PREPARATION

A show cockatiel should be fed a well-balanced, healthy diet all year-round. If a bird is fit and well, it will always look its best. The cockatiel should also be sprayed on a daily basis, as this will help to condition the feathers and will encourage preening. About two months before the show, you will need to examine your cockatiel very carefully. If any feathers are frayed or broken, they can be pulled out, and they will regrow in time for the show.

Show training is also important, as a tiel is judged on deportment as well as its conformation and condition. Train your cockatiel to get used to perching and holding its position. You can reward the bird with a treat. You may find that clicker training (see page 86) is a useful aid, as you can gradually extend the amount of time a cockatiel holds its position by delaying the click. A clicker-trained cockatiel knows that it must earn a click before getting its reward.

If you are exhibiting your cockatiel in a show cage, make sure the birds gets used to this new "home" so that it is happy and settled on show days.

COCKATIEL CRAZY

Linda Greeson of Florida is an avid breeder who exhibits her many cockatiels. Here she describes how she made the transition from novice owner to respected breeder.

"I have always been fond of birds. I had a bright blue parakeet as a child. Then, in 1980, I saw a Yellow Nape Amazon on a TV show, and fell head over heels in love. I decided that I had to have a Parrot like that, and I obtained a beautiful Yellow Nape, which I still have. That was the start of my great interest in all types of birds.

"I started to think about breeding cockatiels. They seemed to be an interesting species, with many beautiful mutations. After learning as much as I could, I found a cockatiel judge who lived in my area and I bought a lovely pair of breeding birds from him. In those days birds were imported to stations in Florida, so I was also able to select birds from those import stations. I chose my original breeding stock from thousands of birds, and that was a huge learning curve for me. Just choosing the birds and learning what to look for was an education.

"Breeding cockatiels is a completely absorbing and exciting hobby. When I first began, I thought a detailed knowledge of genetics and a careful review of each bird's pedigree was enough to make a good breeding judgment. My decisions were made largely at my desk. I soon discovered that a breeding planned on paper does not always work out as expected! Sometimes it can be surprisingly difficult just to get the birds to mate; some cockatiels have minds of their own about accepting a mate! It's quite common for a cockatiel to ignore the hen I've chosen for him while he spends his time actively courting the hen in the adjoining cage. In a case like this, 'wife-swapping' is the only alternative, regardless of careful selection by pedigrees. I set up my breeding pairs several months before providing them with a nesting box, and I usually find some changes to my original plans are necessary.

"I've learned a huge amount over the years and have enjoyed every minute of it. A well-bred animal is, to me, like an oil painting, and I am the artist. It is a challenge to create something extra special, and immensely rewarding when all your careful planning and hard work pays off. That's one of the reasons why exhibiting birds is so much fun. I love showing my birds and seeing how they compare to the accomplishments of other breeders. One of the best moments I've had was when I sold one of my birds to an enthusiastic new breeder. He showed her at a very big show in California and won not only Best in Show for cockatiels, but also Best in Show over all other birds. With an entry of more than 600 birds, that was a real thrill. I have taken Best in Show many times, but to

Continued on page 116

COCKATIEL CRAZY

Continued from page 115

be able to share that moment with someone else was extra special.

"One of my specialties has been breeding for size, which came back to haunt me when I made the move from exhibitor to judge. When I was judging my very first show, some of the exhibitors set up a cage with a huge pigeon in it and presented it to me for judging. Boy, did they get me! Never let it be said that bird people are lacking a sense of humor. I remember another time when we presented a lutino hen to a judge who always seemed to have remarks about the birds' toenails. We had painted the hen's toenails bright red, as a joke. I thought the judge was going to fall on the floor laughing. Eventually, the whole audience started laughing, quickly followed by all the other judges and exhibitors who had come over to see what all the laughter was about. We ended up with 500 people all laughing. It was a show I shall never forget, and neither will the judge—he never made another comment about toenails again!

"Breeding and showing cockatiels is a great passion in my life, and I like to encourage new enthusiasts as much as I can. Showing is a great way to make a start, and it's a wonderful hobby. But it's important to remember that it is also a big responsibility—the future of cockatiels lies in the hands of us breeders."

CHAPTER ELEVEN

HEALTH CARE

Birds have developed over thousands of years, with the knowledge that if they appear sick, they may get eaten! For this reason they hide any signs of ill health until they are very sick.

All birds have a higher metabolic rate than mammals; everything happens faster. They get sick quicker, they die faster. For cockatiels, as they are small birds, this is even more the case.

Birds such as cockatiels eat constantly during the day (as they would in the wild). If a bird does not eat for as little as 48 hours, it can lead to starvation.

One of the first signs of ill health is loss of appetite. Left untreated, an inappetant bird will die rapidly. So detecting underlying disease and recognizing the signs of ill heath are essential.

VETERINARY VISITS

It is a sad reflection that many veterinarians know little about bird medicine. It is certainly very different from cat and dog medicine and does require a different outlook. It is good to do an Internet search or to seek advice from a pet shop as to where you can locate a veterinarian with a particular interest and ability in the care of birds.

You should take your new cockatiel to your veterinarian soon after purchase. He or she can provide advice on many aspects of bird care, as well as give the bird a thorough checkup and possibly test for any high-risk diseases and parasites. Birds living in outside flights should be tested for parasites at least annually.

SIGNS OF ILL HEALTH

When you are assessing a cockatiel, try to look at the whole picture rather than focusing on one aspect of its appearance or behavior. This will help you to evaluate the bird's overall condition and decide if it is in temporary discomfort, such as being cold, or whether it indicates that the cockatiel is unwell. Look for the following signs of ill health:

- Loss or change of appetite (eating more or less).
- Change in the bird's weight. It is advisable to weigh your bird weekly, as a change in weight is often the first sign of illness.
- Alteration in its excrement. There are three portions to a bird's droppings: the dark part being feces, the white part (urates), and the watery part. A watery dropping can mean diarrhea, in which case the dark part is no longer formed, or kidney disease when the feces are still well formed. It will help your veterinarian considerably if you explain which is abnormal in your bird's case. It is important to note that certain food items can dramatically (but temporarily) change the appearance of droppings, as any owner who has given their tiel berries will testify! Bear this in mind when assessing your cockatiel.
- Sleeping more.
- Change in eye shape. Tell your veterinarian if, instead of being round, bright, and shiny, the eye becomes lemon-shaped and sleepy-looking, or if one or both eyes are shut.
- Any abnormal bodily discharges from the nose, mouth, eye, ear, cloaca, or preen gland (on the bottom end of the back where the tail feathers insert).
- Less active.
- Feathers all fluffed up. This is a common sign in a sick bird, which is responding by increasing the depth of its duvet so as to limit the loss of body heat. Bear in mind that a cockatiel will also fluff up its feathers when it is cold and sometimes when it is sleepy.

- Loss or change of voice.
- Wheezing or other abnormal noise as it is breathing.
- Tail bobbing as it breathes.
- Vomiting or regurgitating.
- Delayed crop emptying, or crop leakage from the bird's breast.
- Lameness.
- Wings hanging down.
- Resting on two legs or hanging onto the bars of the cage with its beak. Most healthy birds will rest at times on one foot; if unwell, they rest on two feet; if very sick, they also hang onto the cage bars with their beak, for additional support.
- Change or loss of feathers.
- Bleeding from any feathers or any other site.
- Change of normal perching position, or lying on the cage floor.
- Multiple egg-laying.
- Straining to defecate.

If your bird develops any of these signs, you should contact your veterinarian immediately.

EMERGENCY CARE

As birds are small, with a high metabolic rate, if they are ever seen to be ill, they do require emergency care from an experienced avian veterinarian. Supportive care to be applied prior to getting to see the veterinarian would include the following:

Warmth: Maintain the bird in a quiet, dark, warm place. The temperature may be kept at 75 to 85°F (24 to 29°C). This may be best

A sick cockatiel needs rest, warmth, and often fluid therapy.

achieved by placing the cage in a warm room, perhaps with one side of the cage against a radiator, and a desk light positioned directly above the cage. A towel or similar drape may be placed around the cage, to keep the warmth inside.

Fluid therapy: The bird should be given fluid therapy as a treatment for shock or dehydration. This may be administered by owners at home, so long as they possess a suitable gavage tube and have been instructed as to how to administer the fluid this way. The technique should not be attempted unless the owner has had one-to-one lessons from an experienced breeder or veterinarian.

Controlling blood loss: A cockatiel has a small volume of blood (6.4–12 ml), and can only safely afford to ever lose 10 percent of this:

0.6–1.2 ml, in simpler terms 16–32 drops. So any blood loss is a very serious matter. Any owner finding the bird to be bleeding should pick it up, find the source of bleeding, and apply digital (finger) pressure, until such time as the bleeding is controlled. They should then bring their bird to their avian veterinarian.

UNDERSTANDING DISEASE

Pathogens are defined as organisms that can cause damaging effects to an infected host. In broad terms these are divided into bacteria, viruses, and fungae.

Bacteria

These are organisms made up of just one cell. They are capable of multiplying by themselves, as they have the power to divide. Their shapes vary, and pathologists use these characteristics to separate them into groups.

Bacteria exist everywhere, inside and on our bodies. Most of them are completely harmless and some of them are very useful. But some bacteria can cause diseases, either because they end up in the wrong place in the body, or simply because they are "designed" to invade us. Bacteria can be readily grown in the laboratory. In general terms, bacteria are sensitive to treatment with antibiotics (or disinfectants if in the environment). No one antibiotic is effective against all bacteria, so pathologists may grow a pathogen in the laboratory and test various antibiotics against it to see which is most effective.

Viruses

Viruses are too small to be seen by the naked eye. They can't multiply on their own, so they have to invade a "host" cell and take over its machinery in order to be able to make more virus particles. Viruses consist of genetic materials (DNA or RNA) surrounded by a protective coat of protein. The cells of the mucous membranes, such as those lining the respiratory, gut, or urinogenital tracts, are particularly open to virus attacks because they are not covered by protective skin. In other situations viruses may enter following a breach of the skin, such as following a scratch or bite. There are effective medical treatments for only a small percentage of viruses; in most cases if the host (patient) is to survive this will be as a result of good nursing and nutritional support.

Fungae

Many fungae are ubiquitous (everywhere). They tend to grow when they are provided with a suitable environment in which to do so. They tend to grow on decaying vegetable material and require dampness in order to grow.

The majority of pathogenic effects caused by fungae are related to the toxins that they produce. Fungal infections are typically serious in birds. In many patients the case is too far advanced by the time of initial admission to effect a cure. If treatment is to be given, it will often be required for several months.

COMMON DISEASES

Feathers and skin
There can be different reasons for loss of feathers.

Behavioral disorders
Picking by the mate is usually limited to the back of the head. Feather mutilation syndrome

is reported in cockatiels, where feathers are pecked away and skin damage or infection may be present. Any bird with feather loss (over and above a normal molt) should be taken to a veterinarian. Resolution of these problems can prove complex, lengthy, and expensive.

Vitamin A deficiency
This deficiency, due to an exclusively seed-based diet low in vitamin A, can cause dry, thickened, and itchy skin with poor wound healing. It can lead to feather picking. Diet should be improved, together with supplementary vitamin A.

Parasitic infections
These infections, such as *Cnemidocoptes* spp., usually cause proliferative crusty tissue around the beak and face or feet. This can lead to feather loss around the head due to facial itchiness. *Cnemidocoptes* are mites that are effectively treated with ivermectin supplied by your veterinarian. All in-contact birds should be treated. It is reported that *Giardia* spp. (a gut

Cnemidocoptes results in crusty tissue around the beak.

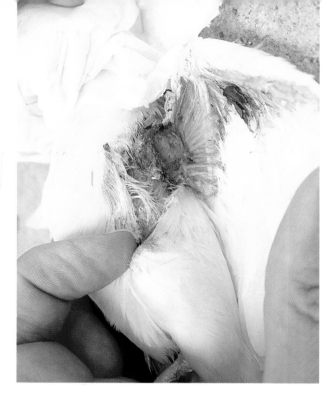

Superficial chronic ulcerative dermatitis (SCUD) is confined to underneath the wing.

parasite) cause feather picking (especially under the wings) due to an allergic reaction, especially in cockatiels in America. This condition can develop into a form of "chronic ulcerative dermatitis" (longstanding ulcerative skin infection), most often found under the wing or either side of the base of the tail. Giardia is a protozoon, which is effectively treated with metronidazole or fenbendazole, available from your veterinarian.

Superficial chronic ulcerative dermatitis (SCUD) is mainly limited to the underneath wing (propatagium), which deteriorates due to picking. This condition usually is caused by *Staphylococcus aureus* (on occasions MRSA) and typically requires a long and patient treatment with sensitive antibiotics (by mouth) together with the topical application of a suitable ointment. Culture and sensitivity tests, by your veterinarian, of the pathogens involved are essential. It may be necessary to prevent wound picking by applying a plastic (Elizabethan-style) or foam collar. Long-term lesions will develop into thickened scar tissue, which can itch and trigger repeated picking.

Viral infections

These include Circovirus and Polyomavirus. Both are contagious, and birds are infected by feather dust or droppings. Feather abnormalities depend on the stage of the feather development.

With respect to Circovirus, very young birds or infected chicks are usually just found dead in the nest, whereas if they are infected a little later, they may die instead of a secondary disease at six months to two years of age. If infected later still, the birds may develop a progressive feather dystrophy that gets progressively worse at each successive molt. Feather changes include bleeding, necrosis, and breakage of the feathers.

Polyomavirus usually affects parakeets but it can also occur in cockatiels. Clinical signs depend also on the age of the bird. Hatchlings have reduced formed down and contour feathers; juveniles show symmetric dystrophic flight and tail feathers ('French molt'). If they are unable to fly, these birds are called "runners." Subcutaneous hemorrhage might also be observed. Unfortunately, there is no effective antiviral treatment. Prevention (hygiene, quarantine) is very important, as well as supportive treatment and also treatment of secondary bacterial and fungal infections.

Normal molt

Cockatiels typically molt once a year over a six-to eight-week period. Molting is triggered by day length, so when pet birds are housed inside with artificial lighting, the trigger for a molt can be delayed. Molting is an active process. A new feather starts to develop; it grows down, pushing the old feather out as it grows. Molting is a period of stress and maximum nutritional demand, so it is advisable to use a proprietary vitamin and mineral supplement at this time. During the molt, a bird will inevitably preen more and itch.

Legs and feet

Bumblefoot (pododermatitis)

This occurs more often in obese birds kept in cages with plastic perches. Malnutrition (vitamin A deficiency), which leads to hyperkeratotic skin, may be also involved as well as healing disorders due to liver disease (a common sequel to obesity).

Birds with bumblefoot should be presented to a veterinarian for treatment, although the owner must appreciate that it is a husbandry-related disease. If the husbandry is not improved, the disease will reoccur, despite the best efforts of the veterinarian. Typically, weight may need to be reduced, perches improved and padding provided on the perch.

Free flight should always be monitored and care must be taken, especially if birds like to sit on top of doors or cupboards.

Fractures (broken legs, toes, wings)

These commonly occur when a door on which a bird has landed is shut. The other common cause is when a bird has overlong toenails. As it tries to fly from the bars of the cage, the nails may catch and hold the bird, while it flaps its wings and attempts to fly away. This twisting and pulling force can often lead to broken legs. Most commonly broken legs involve the lower leg bones (tibiotarsus, tarsometatarsus) and can be repaired by an experienced bird veterinarian. Fractures of the wings are also possible. The bird is often seen with one wing hanging down more than the other, or with the tips of the wing's primary feathers (as they close together on the bird's back in front of the tail) not being symmetrical. Do not ignore such signs, but take the bird to a veterinarian. Orthopedic treatment (surgical or conservative) and pain relief are necessary.

Paralysis

There are reports relating to cockatiel paralysis syndrome, which is seen as weakness of the legs, wings, and beak secondary to malabsorption of

Cracked feet may result if a cockatiel is forced to perch on plastic perches.

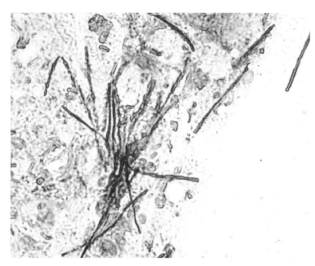

Study under a miscroscope will detect the presence of gastric yeast, also known as megabacteria.

vitamin E/selenium. Treatment with vitamin E/selenium is recommended. Kidney, ovarian, or testicular tumors or infection, or heavy metal (lead or zinc) can cause very similar signs.

Vomiting/regurgitation

Vomiting and regurgitation can occur due to inflammation or infection of the crop. This may be caused by parasites (*Trichomonas* sp.), yeast (*Candida* sp.) or bacterial infection. Diagnosis can be established by a veterinarian, who, after collecting a swab, staining it, and studying it under a microscope, can determine the cause and provide a suitable treatment. A fungal agent (*Ornithogaster macrorhabdus,* otherwise known as gastric yeast, but formally described as megabacteria) can also lead to delayed crop emptying, vomiting, or weight loss. Usually the proventriculus (first part of

the stomach) is affected. Digestion becomes ineffective due to reduction in acid secretion in the stomach, so that weight loss follows. This syndrome was formerly described as "going light syndrome."

Alternatively, vomiting repeatedly (especially by an active, healthy-looking bird) to the owner, another bird, or toy in the cage, can be indicative of courtship behavior. Do not assume the latter is the case, unless you are very experienced, or a veterinarian has checked it out.

Obesity

One big problem for birds kept in captivity can be lack of activity and a fatty energy-dense diet. Wild cockatiels have to fly long distances for foraging. Sitting in a cage having food available ad libitum unfortunately leads to obesity. The owner can check the body condition by carefully feeling the breast muscle with their fingers. Obese birds have a very rounded chest, with no evidence of the bony spine up the middle of the chest; they also tend to have fat deposits under the skin over the muscle (lipoma) of the chest. It might not be obvious when the owner just watches the bird from a distance, since feathers can mask such signs. Fat will also be deposited inside the abdominal cavity, which can lead to breathing difficulties. Obese birds will be disinclined to fly, which further exacerbates their condition. Secondary problems due to obesity include bumblefoot, fatty liver, egg-laying problems, and atherosclerosis. By measuring your bird's weight weekly, any gradual weight increase will be detected and advice can be sought.

Breeding activity

As stated above, birds fed a high-energy diet, or provided with a nest box, will often be stimulated to breed. Unless there is a definite plan and good reason to breed, it is best avoided. In any colony of cockatiels in the wild, there would be nonbreeding birds, so a lack of breeding is not an unnatural situation.

If a hen lays eggs (in an unplanned breeding situation), do not remove them immediately. If they could be fertile and you want her to hatch young, then leave the eggs with her; if this is not the case, leave all the eggs with her until she has been sitting on them for 15 days, then remove them. If you take them earlier, she will simply lay some more.

Once the eggs have been removed, reduce the hen's daylight to eight hours a day (to tell her that it is winter and not a good time to breed), reduce the energy content of her diet, remove any nest or nesting material, and change her to a different cage, or, at worst, move the cage to another location. All these efforts are in an attempt to deter her from laying more eggs. Birds that lay repeated clutches of eggs tend to suffer from egg-laying exhaustion, which will show as weakness of the legs, paralysis, egg binding, or egg peritonitis.

Egg binding

Cockatiels lay eggs until the clutch size is complete (four to six eggs). If these eggs are removed, the female will continue laying. If this goes on, the bird may suffer from exhaustion and nutritional deficiency (such as calcium).

A bird with egg binding (an egg stuck in the oviduct) will look fluffed up and miserable; she may even lie on the cage floor and be unable to get up. Obesity and multiple egg laying are predisposing factors to egg binding. If the eggshell is broken, the risk of oviduct laceration is increased. Such a bird must be presented urgently to an experienced bird veterinarian.

Egg yolk peritonitis

This occurs when a yolk is released from the ovary as usual, but instead of being caught by the infundibulum (funnel) or the oviduct, it falls into the abdomen, leading to peritonitis. This is similar to an ectopic pregnancy in a woman. Egg yolk is an ideal medium for bacterial growth, and, if untreated, this condition can be life-threatening. Birds tend to sit on the bottom of the cage, are fluffed up and lethargic, show abdominal distension, and have breathing difficulties. Any sort of manipulation by the owner should be avoided and the bird should be taken to the veterinarian.

Changes in droppings

Droppings should always be closely monitored by the owner since lots of important information can be achieved. The term "diarrhea" is usually overdiagnosed by the

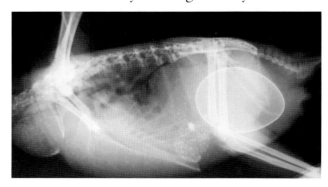

Egg binding is a life-threatening condition.

Roundworm in the gut of a Cockatiel.

owner. One has to distinguish between the feces, urates, and the fluidish part of the droppings. True diarrhea is recognized by soft or runny feces. Bacterial (*E. coli*) enteritis can be a cause. Culture and sensitivity of a fresh fecal sample or cloacal swab is necessary for an effective treatment. Parasitic infestation is seen most commonly in birds in outside flights. Fecal examination may reveal the presence of roundworms (*ascaridia*), tapeworms, and protozoa (such as *coccidia*).

Undigested seeds in the feces are an indication of Proventricular Dilatation Syndrome (PDS). Larger Parrots most commonly suffer from this condition, but cockatiels can be affected. It is believed that a virus infects the bird, damaging the nerves that supply the muscles of the gut wall. Inflammation of nerve cells results in a decrease of gastrointestinal motility. Clinical signs include vomiting, weight loss, lethargy, and undigested seeds. Central nervous signs have also been reported. Treatment (nonsteroidal anti-inflammatory drugs) can be

administered to control the effects of the disease (and achieve a good quality of life), although a cure is unlikely.

If the fecal element is well formed, but the white or fluid part are very runny, this is termed polyuria. High-water (fruity) diets can cause such runny droppings and be quite a normal physiological effect. Kidney diseases as well as diabetes mellitus should be considered in constantly wet droppings.

Urates, which are the insoluble particles forming the nitrogen waste, should be white. Yellow discoloration can indicate liver disease (hepatitis, fatty liver). Green urates can be connected with lead intoxication, reduced food intake, or liver disease. Since cockatiels enjoy chewing (like all other Parrots), sources containing heavy metal (lead, zinc) need to be removed from the bird's surroundings.

Respiratory disease

Teflon toxicity

Teflon (polytetrafluoroethylene) is a compound found in nonstick cookware, grill sheets, in some self-clean ovens, under some irons, in some ironing board covers, as a water-proofing agent on some outdoor clothes, as a toughening agent in some household paints, as a black matte finish over the bulb of some heat lamps, as well as in other situations. If, in any circumstance, such a material becomes overheated, it will release a highly toxic substance that will very rapidly lead to the death of any in-contact birds. The typical scenario would be: someone in an apartment building burning their frying pan, and every parkaeet in the whole building dying in the next 10 minutes. There are few clinical signs, save that birds died rapidly, typically soon after food was cooked for human consumption.

Psittacosis (Chlamydophila)

It is reported that 75–90 percent of cockatiel studs are infected with this disease. If your bird suffers from conjunctivitis and/or rhinitis (any eye or nose discharge or sneezing), then psittacosis should be considered. The disease is caused by *Chlamydophila* spp., which is a zoonotic disease: it can cause infection, disease, and, very rarely, death in humans. So infected birds, whether they look ill, or appear perfectly healthy, can transmit the disease to humans and vice versa. Humans may suffer severe pneumonia.

Apart from conjunctivitis and rhinitis, clinical signs include lethargy, anorexia, watery droppings, and yellow urates. Central nervous signs (such as tremors, falling off the perch, inco-ordination) might also develop. Untreated birds may die from dehydration and hypoglycemia. The pathogen is shed in the feces and spread in feather and fecal dust—in the air. Birds are infected after eating or breathing in the agent.

Diagnosis is possible by detecting antibodies in the blood or antigen in the conjunctiva, oral cavity, and feces. Birds can be effectively treated. Owners of any new cockatiel are advised to have the bird tested for this disease. Humans over 45, or those who are pregnant, are most likely to suffer severe disease. Typically, if humans are infected, they are not at danger as long as the doctors know what is wrong so the right treatment can be given. Clinical signs in humans include: pneumonia, swollen lymph nodes, flulike symptoms, headaches, night sweats, or liver disease.

ZOONOTIC INFECTIONS

There are a number of diseases that, under rare conditions, can be transmitted to humans and cause mild to serious, even on occasions fatal, infections. Viruses include Avian Influenza, West Nile Virus, Newcastle's Disease, Q Fever, fungus, such as Cryptococcus, and bacteria such as *Chlamydophila psittaci* (which causes psitticosis), *Salmonella* spp., *Campylobacter* spp., *Mycobaterium avium*, *Yersinia* spp., and *E. coli*.

The prevalence of any such disease will vary with respect to the source of the bird and the region in which you live. At the time of your initial health screen with your veterinarian, you should discuss the issue of zoonotic infections, so that he or she can screen for those that are relevant. In most cases this will only be psitticosis, unless your bird is known to be actively suffering from one of the other diseases, in which case additional care will be required.

SUMMARY

Keeping cockatiels is a rewarding hobby since they are enjoyable pets and have a good life expectancy. However, one needs to acknowledge that the appropriate humane housing and care of these birds is generally more complex than that needed for a cat or a dog. In addition, birds tend to hide the signs of clinical diseases until they are very sick, which makes it challenging for the owner and veterinarian to react in time, to save the sick bird. Therefore, it is up to the owner to bring the bird to the veterinarian when first purchased, as well as returning for annual health checks. Owners should also monitor the birds closely and seek advice at the first sign of ill health.

USEFUL ADDRESSES

UNITED STATES

American Cockatiel Society
9527 60th Lane North
Pinellas Park, FL 34666
www.acstiels.com

National Cockatiel Society
PO Box 1363
Avon, CT 06001-1363
www.cockatiels.org

American Federation of Aviculture
PO Box 56218
Phoenix, AZ 85079-6218
www.afabirds.org

Association of Avian Veterinarians
Central Office,
PO Box 811720
Boca Raton, FL 33481
http://www.aav.org/

Cockatiel Rescue
4208 Ridgerunner Road, NW
Albuquerque, NM 87114
www.cockatielrescue.org

CANADA

British Columbia Avicultural Society
11784-90th Ave.
North Delta, British Columbia
V4C 3H6

The Canadian Avicultural Society
32 Dronmore Ct.
Willowdale, Ontario M2R 2H5

Canadian Parrot Association
Pine Oaks R. R. #3
St. Catharines, Ontario
L2R 6P9

WEB SITES
http://www.petbirdpage.com/breed.asp?breed=cocktiel